A LITTLE NIGHTMUSIC

Books by Samuel Chotzinoff

A LITTLE NIGHTMUSIC

TOSCANINI: AN INTIMATE PORTRAIT

A LOST PARADISE

EROICA

For TED PATRICK

intimate conversations with

JASCHA HEIFETZ · VLADIMIR HOROWITZ

GIAN CARLO MENOTTI · LEONTYNE PRICE

RICHARD RODGERS · ARTUR RUBINSTEIN

ANDRÉS SEGOVIA

drawings by

MME OLGA KOUSSEVITZKY

A LITTLE NIGHTMUSIC

by Samuel Chotzinoff

HARPER & ROW, PUBLISHERS

New York, Evanston, and London

CONTENTS

JASCHA HEIFETZ

CARRYING HIS VIOLIN in its oblong case—he will not trust anyone but himself with his precious instrument—Heifetz walks briskly into his classroom at the University of Southern California.

"Good morning, boys and girls," he calls out cheerfully; then, "Ladies and gentlemen," he corrects himself. The greeting is perhaps a bit too hearty. In its inflection there is something of self-consciousness, and something promissory of pedagogic severity.

"Good morning, Mr. Heifetz," the class responds even more cheerfully than their master; and in their response there is a touch of restlessness, a premonition of their teacher's exactitude, of inordinate demands he will make on them.

The great violinist takes out his violin, gently removes the silk kerchief in which it rests, sits down at his desk and calls out the name of a student. A tall, slim young woman, very agreeable to look at, advances, violin in hand.

"What have you prepared?" Heifetz asks.

She stands before him flustered, revealing in her stance and her motions tiny evidences of nervousness. The rest of the class, three youths and a young lady of fourteen, sitting ranged against the wall, watch her narrowly.

"Chausson's *Poème,*" the student answers.

"Would you like to warm up on a few scales?" Heifetz inquires with an innocent air. Scales are difficult to play in tune. The young lady, aware that the innocent-seeming query is a command rather than the offer of a choice, murmurs that yes, she *would* like to warm up on scales. The pupils against the wall lean forward in apprehension.

"Well!" Heifetz, smiling, says. "This is one of the rare times when I hear a *choice* of scales. I should commend you for bravery. How about a G flat minor scale in fingered octaves?"

There is an audible gasp from the class, for fingered octaves are the very devil to play. The young woman, dismayed, is speechless for a moment. Then she sighs and murmurs, "Oh, Mr. Heifetz!" Mr. Heifetz, unrelenting, uncommunicative, is silent. The class looks politely away. The young woman puts her violin under her chin and gives her teacher a last, pleading look.

"Don't worry," he says, "you'll survive." The pupil negotiates the precarious scale gingerly several times, and at the end the teacher calls out encouragingly, "You see, you're still in one piece. And now the *Poème.*"

She begins the *Poème* slowly, but with an assurance that was wanting in the scale in fingered octaves. After a few bars Heifetz taps the desk with a pencil, and the young woman stops.

"The *Poème,*" he says, "can be played in ten or twelve minutes. I once heard it played in eighteen minutes, allowing the customers to have a snooze. For myself, I'd rather finish it *before* the audience falls asleep."

The pupil continues, but at a faster pace. Heifetz cocks an attentive ear. "Don't slide into base," he warns at one point. The pupils laugh, and he smiles, obviously pleased at their reaction to his knowledge of baseball. Again he raps with his pencil, takes up his violin and tunes it.

"It is important to look at the music once in a while," he says. "I began looking at the music some years ago and I was horrified at the mistakes I had been making. Now, at this moment in the music, the violin is fighting against a full orchestra playing *fortissimo*. You must give all you can or you won't be heard. Like this." And he plays the passage with great energy and fullness of tone. The class, their faces aglow with admiration, scribble notes on their scores. The young woman then plays the passage with all the strength she can command, and the teacher nods his approval. She finishes the *Poème* to the generous applause of her fellow students and resumes her seat against the wall.

As I listened to the *Poème* of Chausson my memory went back to the year 1920, to a rehearsal on the stage of the Salle Gaveau in Paris. Jascha Heifetz was playing the Chausson *Poème* in front of a full symphony orchestra led by Paul Paray. Madame Chausson, the widow of the composer, and I were the only listeners in the hall. Madame Chausson's interest in the performance was, understandably, an emotional one. Mine was, at the moment, rather practical. Just before he walked out on the stage I had bet Heifetz ten thousand francs that when he came to the climax of the piece where, as he warned his pupil, "the violin is fighting against a full orchestra playing *fortissimo*," the full orchestra would swamp his playing, as it had swamped the playing of every other violinist I had ever heard. The passage arrived, and, to my astonishment,

5

the solo violin soared clear above the fortissimo sound of the orchestra. I had lost the bet. And I had to find what consolation I could in the demonstration I had heard. The thing, difficult as it might be, could be done.

"Who is next?" Heifetz now asks, and a young Lebanese with liquid eyes and jet-black hair steps forth.

"And what have you prepared?" he is asked, and he answers, "Two Paganini caprices and the Brahms *Concerto*. Which shall I play first?"

"The Bach *Chaconne*," Heifetz says blandly. His face is blank, deadpan, as it is when he comes out on the stage of Carnegie Hall. The pupils fidget uncomfortably. The Lebanese youth looks bewildered, incredulous. "The *Chaconne?*" he says, as if he hadn't heard aright.

"The *Chaconne*," Heifetz calmly iterates. The youth, slowly recovering from the unexpected demand, smiles wryly, fishes out the score of the *Chaconne* from his music case, places it on the stand, gives his violin a confidential tuning with the tip of his bow and begins to play. He is brought to a stop after a dozen bars.

"You know," Heifetz says, rising and reaching for his violin, "or if you don't you *should* know, that the *Chaconne* is a dance. It happens to be a slow dance, but it is still a dance. Its rhythm is something like this." Heifetz walks stately and relentlessly in three-quarter time in front of his pupil. It is a ceremonial walk, slow, but without hesitation. "I dance quite slowly," he is saying, "but strictly in time. I don't hesitate between the third and first beat as you often do. You play slowly but jerkily, not at all in time. It should go like this." He puts his violin under his chin and begins the *Chaconne*, walking the while and suiting the rhythm of his playing to his steps. He stops playing and the Lebanese takes over. He plays in tempo,

6

slow and measured. His teacher says it is much better now, and a happy glow suffuses the pupil's eager face.

The *Chaconne* is given a thorough going over. The slightest flaw is noticed and corrected. The tapping pencil is ever on the alert. "Serenely," says the teacher at one point, "quietly, gently, musingly, like this," and out comes his own violin, and the great violinist plays the variation quietly, gently, musingly, in his own seemingly easy fashion. The Lebanese watches the masterly bow and the steely, now velvet-tipped fingers with awe, and the other pupils busily mark their scores. At the end of the piece Heifetz says to the young man, "You can finish with or without a trill. There is no trill in the original manuscript. But if you feel like a trill go right ahead and play one. It's a matter of choice. I don't play one." The young man prudently decides to dispense with a trill. At last the *Chaconne* is finished. "Not bad, not bad," Heifetz comments. The Lebanese takes it as a great compliment and stammers his thanks. He is quickly disillusioned. "But watch your bow, it jumps around too much. If you're not careful it will fly out the window some day. Or I may take it away from you."

The class is dismissed and Heifetz and I drive back to Beverly Hills, where he lives in a rambling one-story house perched on the top of one of the sandy peaks of that expensive and expanding neighborhood. We make the perilous ascent, Heifetz deftly maneuvering his steel-gray Bentley. When we reach his garage he presses a button on his dashboard, the garage door rises as by magic and we drive in. "Marvelous!" I murmur, though I've seen other garages so equipped. But I know my wonderment will please Jascha, who has never lost his delight in gadgets or his fondness for surprising others with them.

I have known Heifetz for forty-three years. He was

7

sixty-three on February the second of this year. (Fritz Kreisler was also born on February the second; the two violinists used to exchange birthday greetings.) He is somewhat stocky, but is still pink-cheeked, has prominent cheekbones, blue eyes and a finely shaped nose. He may be called handsome. In his younger days he was remarkable for the fine proportions of his figure and his classic features. In a photograph taken when he was twenty-six, he looks as slim and as handsome as a movie star. The picture is inscribed to "dear tactless Pauline," his sister, and the dedication hints at a charming relationship between the two and a difference in their characters. Jascha is reserved and correct; Pauline is outspoken. Yet the pair have maintained a close friendship since their childhood, when they both studied at the St. Petersburg Conservatory and played violin and piano sonatas together in Professor Leopold Auer's master class and at home for their parents and friends. When time permitted, they went together to the Hermitage museum, the Museum of Natural History, the Zoological Gardens, and sometimes they were taken to concerts and to the opera at the Marinsky Theatre. Their parents felt instinctively, for they themselves had had no formal education, that an artist would be greatly benefited by a knowledge of what had been done in science and art. So the two children enjoyed the culture of Czarist Russia, studied French, German, history, geography and arithmetic with private tutors at home, and practiced their instruments assiduously.

Their leisure moments—there were not many—were devoted to games of the horseplay variety, which did much to relieve the rigors and tensions of their otherwise studious existence. Jascha was made to practice not less than four

hours each day and often as many as six. There was no
time for him to form friendships with fellow students and
boys of the neighborhood. He was not permitted to go in for
sports where his invaluable, extraordinary hands might be
in jeopardy. But he managed to have "fun," he confesses,
at home, where he maintained a kind of feudal suzerainty
over his sisters, Pauline and Elza. At the conservatory, in
Auer's class, and in piano and composition classes, he was
a model of respectful juvenility. At home, when his parents
were away, he could unbend and exact obedience from his
helpless younger sisters. And when their obedience was lax
or not forthcoming, the master of the violin did not hesitate
to apply force. Indeed, the girls could hardly wait for their
little brother to take off on his occasional tours. It was their
parents' belief, and also Professor Auer's, that the boy violinist must grow accustomed to playing to audiences early
in life, a belief which his sisters devoutly shared, but for
reasons of their own.

Playing the violin superbly was, from the very beginning, second nature to Jascha, as unremarkable, as uncomplicated as walking and breathing. Therefore, to be outstanding, to shine in what for him was a significant way,
became a pressing need. Its manifestations were and still are
touchingly naïve. Quite unaware of, or unimpressed with,
his acknowledged status as the world's greatest violinist, he
has always sought recognition for extraneous accomplish-
ments, such as being well dressed, expert at ping-pong and
tennis, and the repository of such general information as
the names of our states, the capitals thereof, the opening
theme of a Beethoven quartet, the winner of a champion-
ship tennis match between America and Australia in the
early twenties, and the like.

9

Generating and maintaining an air of mystery is another sure way to create an impression, and as a child Jascha laid the foundation for a reputation for mystery which he has maintained to the present day. At a tender age the boy discovered in his sisters certain frailties, particularly curiosity, which he was quick to take advantage of. Under his bed he placed a tin box, securely locked, the contents of which none but he had seen. It became agony for the little Heifetz girls not to know what their brother kept in that mysterious box. And one day, when he was playing out of town, they could hold out no longer. With a hammer and pliers they forced the lock, expecting to find a large collection of jewels. To their astonishment and disappointment, the box was crammed with an assortment of bottle caps. When the virtuoso returned and found his treasure chest opened and its mystery dissipated, his childish wrath was extreme. Under torture the girls confessed and were duly punished. The bottle caps were discarded and Jascha began collecting something else, the nature of which he never divulged. From then on, the tin box accompanied the violinist on all his trips away from home.

He was, at the time of the bottle-cap disclosure, about nine years old. By then he was a veteran of the concert stage and a name in Russia. Many years later, in New York, I heard Heifetz and Harpo Marx, the zany and usually silent comic, exchange reminiscences of their childhood. "And how old were you, Jascha, when you first began to earn your living?" Harpo asked, and Heifetz promptly replied, "Six." "I suppose," the comic said with the utmost gravity, "before then you were just a bum."

In truth, Heifetz was anything but a bum "before then,"

for he was three when his father bought him a quarter-size violin and began to teach him, his father being himself a violinist who earned his living by playing in cafés and music halls. Jascha was born in Vilna in 1901. In 1908 the Heifetz family moved to Leningrad, then called St. Petersburg, and Jascha entered the St. Petersburg Conservatory, studying first with the Armenian teacher Nalboldian and later with Professor Leopold Auer. When he was eight, Jascha made his first appearance with a symphony orchestra. Clad in a Fauntleroy suit of velvet—the uniform of child prodigies—the little boy, while awaiting his turn, fell asleep in an armchair in the artists' room. When he was called, his mother woke him up, straightened his clothes and combed his hair; his father tuned his violin for him (it is difficult for a child to manipulate the pegs of a violin); and the boy walked out on the stage with the assurance of a professional and played the Mendelssohn *Concerto* to perfection. At ten he appeared with orchestras in Odessa and Kiev. At eleven he played the Tchaikovsky *Concerto* at the Gewandhaus in Leipzig under Artur Nikisch, and in Vienna under the Russian conductor Wassilly Saffonoff. These appearances and some solo concerts were too few to interfere with his education at home, and they inured him to the presence of audiences. But when Jascha's fame spread to America, and American concert managers besieged his mother with offers of fabulous sums, she turned a deaf ear.

As we cross the courtyard of his eyrie in Beverly Hills I tell Jascha that he was indeed fortunate in his parents and his teachers, all of whom took a long-range view of his career and permitted nothing to get in the way of the normal progress of his musical development. And as we sit

11

down in his studio, a sort of roundhouse set apart from the main house, I point out that very few *Wunderkinder* ever realize their early promise.

"You know," Heifetz says, "child prodigism—if I may coin a word" (he loves to coin words) "—is a disease which is generally fatal. I was among the few who had the good fortune to survive. But you are right. I had the advantage of a great teacher in Professor Auer, and a family which instinctively had a high regard for music, very good taste and a horror of mediocrity. My parents' ambition was for me to learn to play the violin as perfectly as my talent allowed, to provide the best musical instruction obtainable, and to make me practice hard during childhood and early youth, when fingers are most pliant and a feeling for beauty is more easily instilled.

"From what I have heard of the usual parents of child prodigies," he went on, "I wouldn't hesitate to place the responsibility for the large mortality, musically speaking, among gifted children on their fathers and mothers. Most of these parents are so overawed by their good fortune that they lose their balance and take whatever short cuts are offered them to fame and fortune. So they send their poor little tots out into the competitive world at a time when they should be working hard at home, shielded from flattery and exploitation.

"I suppose the rigors of the routine my parents imposed on me were at the cost of what we call a normal childhood. It's true that I wasn't allowed to play all the rough-and-tumble games children enjoy. I had to wait a few years before I enjoyed," and here Jascha smiled, "a delayed childhood, when I could do all the risky and dangerous things I was forbidden to do as a child."

12

I had been a witness of Heifetz's "delayed" childhood. He was nineteen when, as his accompanist, I spent some weeks with him and his family at their beach house in Narragansett Pier, and I was surprised to find him taking full part in the reckless activities of the teenagers around him. He raced his sports car and, disregarding the possible harm to his hands, he played tennis, golf and baseball, handled firearms and rapiers and led the strenuous life of one who aspires to be a professional athlete.

Jascha laughed at my recollection of those reckless days. "I was even more shocked," I told him, "at your mother's outward indifference to your pranks, and I remembered remonstrating with her for permitting them. Many times you were in danger of breaking one or more of your precious fingers or your wrists, to say nothing of losing your life racing your car against those of your equally reckless but more expendable companions. But your mother laughed at my fears (years later she confessed to the anxiety you had caused her) and did nothing to restrain you; wisely, perhaps, since she knew you felt quite emancipated and that you wouldn't have heeded her in any case. So she thought it best, since she couldn't stop you, to let you have your way and to conceal her fears.

"She was a remarkable woman. I remember, too, around that time a remark of hers which impressed me by its sagacity. She and I were alone one day discussing your forthcoming tour. From the adjoining room came sounds of 'horseplay,' of laughing and screaming, of overturned furniture, where you and your sisters were knocking each other and all other movable objects about. My face must have expressed astonishment at the juvenile antics of the world's most famous violinist. Your mother noticed it and

13

patted my arm reassuringly. 'I am so happy,' she said with emotion, 'that my children are a little stupid. Let them enjoy before life catches up with them.' "

Jascha, who had never heard this story, was visibly moved. "Yes," he agreed, "my mother *was* a remarkable woman. She was impartial in her treatment of her three children. She was, in fact, anything but a doting mother. I could never get a swelled head from anything she ever said to me. She was musical by nature, and she was very critical about my playing. She was moderate in her praise and unsparing in her censure. She liked the playing of other concert violinists, and she adored Kreisler, or 'Kraysler' as she called him, and never missed any of his concerts if she could help it. She admired Josef Hoffmann, Rachmaninoff and Chaliapin, and during the years we lived in Leningrad she took me often to hear them. In this country, among conductors, her heart belonged to Toscanini. She always took his part in any little arguments the Maestro and I might have. And he adored her. I guess she had a great influence on me. Not that she was able to express herself about music. She had been brought up in a small Russian village, had never had the benefit of an education, and she heard her first concert after she married my father and went to live in Vilna.

"My father, too, was severe with me. He was a very good teacher, because when he handed me over to a certain Malkin, then the best violin teacher in Vilna, I already had, as a child of five, a pretty good technical foundation. In fact, soon after, Malkin arranged my first public appearance. Yes, my father was strict with me when I was his pupil, and when I studied with Malkin and later with Auer he superintended my practicing. He never let me get

14

by with anything. He hovered over me. 'The fourth finger, Jaschinka!' he would exclaim; or 'Down bow! Down bow! The Professor wants a down bow.' You remember, even when I was a grown man he would grab my arm as I was about to walk out on the stage and beg me not to forget this, that or the other in fingering or bowing."

"He was very proud of you," I said. "He never tired of telling me how wonderful you were."

"Well, he was careful not to praise me to my face," Jascha said. "And I am grateful to him about his concern about bowing and fingering. Believe me, if I did learn to play the violin well, it was—aside from the enormous debt I owe to Professor Auer—due to my father's watchfulness and patience. On the purely musical side I have my mother to thank for her exquisite taste and her impersonal attitude to my playing. I think no budding artist ever had such a standoffish, matter-of-fact family. For me that was all to the good."

I remember well the atmosphere at after-concert suppers for Jascha at his mother's house. If the concert had gone well, and most of Jascha's concerts were practically faultless, nothing beyond a few expressions of measured approval was offered the artist by members of his family. But on those rare evenings when Jascha had not been at his best, a condition hardly noticeable to any but trained and experienced violinists, not a word of praise was vouchsafed. Nor, used as he was from childhood to his family's impersonal attitude to his playing, did he show any displeasure when praise was not forthcoming.

Jascha, still musing about his mother—she died in 1947—and the influence she had on his life, goes back again, in memory, to his childhood.

"You know, when I was a little boy my mother turned down tempting offers from European and American managers. She let me play occasionally in public, of course, with the consent of Professor Auer. But she kept me at home most of the time. There was so much to do. I had to learn Hebrew, because my maternal grandfather was very religious. My parents gave a party for my Bar Mitzvah, and I made a speech in Hebrew. That night I played the Glazunov *Concerto* in public, with Glazunov himself conducting. It was a great day for me and my family.

"In summer we would follow Professor Auer wherever he held classes. He always chose cool places. So in the summer of 1914 we went along with him to Loeschwitz, a suburb of Dresden, and it was there that the outbreak of the First World War caught us. We were, of course, enemy aliens in Germany; we were ordered to Berlin to be registered as such, and there my parents had to report each day. By a lucky chance Count von Moltke, the German Chief of Staff, was a music lover. He had heard me play and liked me. On the strength of this my mother asked him for a safe-conduct for us to neutral Finland, and this the Count was kind enough to give us. When we got to Finland, railroad transportation to Russia was not available. It was the dead of winter, and we had to travel in a sleigh over frozen lakes. It was great fun for us children, but we arrived in Leningrad half frozen. At home I resumed my studies and played many war benefits. In 1917 the Revolution broke out. We were very excited about the new liberal government and about the handsome and eloquent Alexander Kerensky who was its leader.

"By then I was sixteen and Professor Auer said I was ready for a career. An offer from an American manager came about that time, and my mother accepted it. The contract called for twenty concerts at a fee of five hundred dollars each. Things were looking up in Russia, and we had every intention of coming back after our American tour. But my father prudently hid all the money we had—about forty thousand rubles—in the heel of one of his shoes, just in case. We made the long train journey through Siberia to Vladivostok. From there we went by boat to Japan, and then on to San Francisco, where we were met by our American manager. None of the family spoke a word of English.

"Well, two months after we left Russia the Bolsheviks took over, and father's forty thousand rubles became overnight worthless pieces of paper. Mother decided to make America our home. My sisters were packed off to Newton, near Boston, to live with one of Father's relatives and attend public school, and, I suspect, to be out of the way during the preparations for my New York debut."

I didn't know Jascha at the time, but I was present at his memorable debut at Carnegie Hall. His fame had preceded him and the Hall was packed. Every musician who could get in was there. The sixteen-year-old violinist seemed the most unconcerned of all the people in the Hall as he walked out on the stage and proceeded to give an exhibition of such extraordinary virtuosity and musicianship as had not previously been heard in that historic auditorium. From every violinistic and musical standpoint, the recital was perfection itself.

The critics next day went all out in their praise of Jascha Heifetz, but the recipient of those rave reviews did not read them at the time. The reasons were two. First, he couldn't read English, and, second, his mother always kept press notices from him for fear that praise might give him a sense of his own importance. It was not till thirty years later that Heifetz saw the reviews of his American debut, when, after his mother's death, a great collection of his press notices from his earliest childhood on was discovered in a closet in her room.

For Jascha his New York debut was just another concert, and he was unaware that he had become overnight the musical idol of America. Such were the demands to hear him that in that first year he made thirty appearances in New York alone. To his manager he was a gold mine, a circumstance which Mrs. Heifetz soon began to deplore. For while he was legally within his rights, she felt that the manager should have renegotiated the contract to give her son a more equitable share of what he was earning. Her suggestions for a new settlement were ignored, but the manager soon discovered that even in the matter of American legality he was no match for her. In good time she pointed out to him that Jascha was still a minor, and that as such he might choose not to play at all. The manager, awed by her astuteness, reluctantly renegotiated.

In the meantime young Heifetz had learned to speak and write English and had become aware of the freedoms and pleasures enjoyed by American youths of his age. To his elder sister who was living on the outskirts of Boston he confided, by mail and in Russian, his delight in his adopted country, his hopes and his aspirations. The latter were, it seems, mostly of a mundane nature. "Imagine!" he tells her enthusiastically. "Tomorrow I am to be fitted for my first tail coat! I can hardly wait. And when you come to New York for Christmas we have been promised tickets to the Metropolitan Opera House! You will, of course, get an evening dress! Won't that be marvelous?" The visit to the

Metropolitan duly took place. Resplendent in his first tail coat and accompanied by his fifteen-year-old sister, radiant in her first evening gown, Jascha sat in a box in the Golden Horseshoe. Armed with opera glasses the young man kept his eyes riveted on the stage, quite unaware that he himself was the target of many opera glasses.

When he played in Chicago to a house that had been sold out on the day of the announcement of the concert, he was so besieged by admirers in the artists' room that he had the greatest difficulty getting to his waiting automobile. The following afternoon Fritz Kreisler gave a recital. Mrs. Heifetz had bought a box and we went to hear him. Mrs. Heifetz sat spellbound throughout the recital, and her famous son, sitting discreetly behind her, was completely absorbed in the playing of his great colleague. And, indeed, Kreisler that afternoon was at his very best. He began with the Mendelssohn *Concerto*. And when it was over Mrs. Heifetz turned to her son with a look that said as plainly as words, "Try and beat that!" Like his mother, Jascha always remained a Kreisler devotee. And when later Kreisler met with an accident that incapacitated him for several years, Jascha, out of admiration and respect, played no Kreisler compositions until the beloved violinist had recovered and was able to play them himself. Nor did Jascha make any public announcement of a decision which deprived him of a popular portion of the violin repertoire.

We leave the studio and go to the main house. Heifetz's addiction to precision is manifest in the symmetry and orderliness of the various rooms. Expensive paintings are on the walls—Dufy, Soutine, Rouault, Gluckmann, Rubin. Books are everywhere in evidence, placed in the order of their subject matter and thoroughly catalogued. There is a concealed bar in the hallway and through a sliding window Heifetz passes drinks to people in the larger of two living rooms. Mixing drinks is, like most everything else with Heifetz, a rite.

Heifetz now shoves me a drink through the sliding window, makes one for himself and comes and sits beside me. "You have a fine class at the university," I tell him. "Who would have thought in the old days that you would teach the violin?"

"Well," he says, "Professor Auer once predicted it, and I've always had the possibility in the back of my mind."

"And you seem to enjoy it," I add.

"I've always enjoyed what I did, except practicing. That I enjoy now. The reason, I suppose, was that I had practiced so hard as a child. After I came to America my one aim, it seems to me now, was to enjoy myself. Do you remember the first time we went to Paris? My thoughts then were not on the debut I came to make but on seeing the Folies-Bergère."

I did remember. The very first thing we did on arriving in Paris was to buy two tickets for the Folies-Bergère for the following evening. But the next morning Jascha's French manager showed up with what he considered a piece of luck. An American lady had telephoned him and engaged Jascha to play at her house that night. Jascha shook his head. "Sorry I can't accept," he said to the manager. "We're going to the Folies-Bergère."

"The Folies-Bergère!" cried the manager in utter astonishment. "But you can go to the Folies some other night. This is a paid concert."

"Oh, but we already have our tickets," Jascha said, "and

20

they're hard to get. Besides, I *want* to go to the Folies-Bergère and I do *not* want to play a private concert." Suddenly an idea struck him. "What fee did you quote?" he asked his manager.

"The full fee, fifteen hundred dollars."

Forty-two years ago, fifteen hundred dollars was a considerable fee for a concert artist. In Paris it was unheard of.

"I'll tell you what to do," Jascha exclaimed. "Call her up and say you made a mistake. Tell her my fee for a private concert is double. Ask three thousand. That'll quiet her, and we can go to the Folies-Bergère."

The manager, shaking his head, reluctantly went to the telephone in the next room. After a while he came back, almost running.

"She is willing to pay three thousand!" he announced triumphantly. "You are to come to her house at eight o'clock tonight, no dress."

Jascha looked crushed. "Well," he said apologetically to me, "*perhaps* we'll get through early enough to catch some part of the show." And so it turned out. At eight we were in the rich American's living room. She was a deaf old lady, and she held a trumpet to her ear as we played. Our audience consisted of three people—the rich American, her young niece and a bearded professor of the violin from the Paris Conservatory. After we had played for half an hour or so our eccentric hostess expressed satisfaction, thanked Jascha, shook his hand and said she hoped he would come again sometime and play for her. We hastened downstairs, hailed a cab and were in time for at least three-quarters of the Folies-Bergère, which we enjoyed immensely.

We had come to Paris from London, where Heifetz

21

was to make his debut. He was at once enamored of England and its people, and he decided to become as English as he possibly could. He adopted the long "a" in speaking, and, distasteful as it was, he drank highballs without ice and with the addition of tepid water. He patronized the most fashionable tailor in Savile Row and himself supervised the fittings; and on a certain Sunday he and I paraded up and down Piccadilly in cutaways, striped pants, toppers, canes and gloves—the latter not worn, but carried nonchalantly in one hand. We shopped, we strolled, we visited places of note, we drove to the races in a Rolls-Royce with a liveried chauffeur, and ragamuffins ran after our car and shouted the traditional plea, "Throw out your moldering coppers," which we did, scattering pennies along the route. The one thing Heifetz did not do was practice the violin. His London debut, next to the New York in importance, was now only some days away, and Jascha hadn't once opened his violin case. Finally, after strong representations on my part—I was ten years older than Heifetz and believed myself more sensible—he grudgingly ran over a few scales on the three remaining days.

When, therefore, on the night of his debut Jascha stood in the wings of Queen's Hall, about to walk out on the stage, I was hardly surprised when he turned to me with a worried look. It was the first time I had seen him show anxiety before a concert.

"You're worried?" I asked sympathetically, trying to anticipate him.

"I am," he replied. "I've a feeling that one leg of my pants" (he probably said "trousers") "is shorter than the other. Please look." He turned around, I looked and saw he was right. "The left one is a bit short," I said, greatly

22

relieved. He manipulated his "braces" and brought the legs of his trousers into alignment. Now he no longer looked worried; he walked onto the stage with his habitual serenity and slightly self-conscious diffidence and played with the finesse and accuracy of one who had practiced many hours for many weeks. George Bernard Shaw, who was among the audience, sent Jascha a note the next day, which said, in effect, that he had never in his life heard playing so irritatingly perfect, and that, in consequence, he had spent a sleepless night.

"I must admit I took tremendous chances. Nowadays, in order to keep fit I like to practice at least an hour each day," Heifetz says as if one hour is for him quite sufficient. "And, because they're young, I expect my pupils to practice several hours a day." I do not say it to him, but I believe that a technique like Heifetz's can neither be acquired nor maintained by assiduous practice. I believe that he was born with a hand and finger formation magnificently geared to the nature of the violin. Equally exceptional are his musicality and his faultless ear, and it is the combination of these natural endowments that makes Jascha Heifetz the unique performer he is.

His mind is still on his recollections of his youth.

"Remember," he says, "the morning in Rome when I went walking alone and stopped at a fraudulent picture dealer's shop, and was persuaded to buy what he said were ten little 'Titians'? And when I returned to our hotel and proudly told you about it you scolded me for my foolishness, demanded the dealer's address, ran to him and threatened to call the police if he didn't immediately return the check for a thousand dollars which I had given him as a down payment. That was amusing." (I hadn't found it amusing at the time, though now I laugh with Jascha at the recollection.) "And will you ever forget that evening in Paris after one of my recitals when you and I, still dressed in white tie and tails, had a champagne supper in my suite at Claridge's, and we laughed and laughed for no reason at all, and fell asleep in our chairs? And then suddenly you heard a knocking and woke up, hardly knowing where you were and what had happened. You staggered to the door and there stood a lady who claimed she had an appointment with me for ten in the morning. To your surprise it *was* ten in the morning! You asked her to wait outside, woke me up—which took some time—rushed me into my bedroom and helped me undress and dress. Now what could we have laughed so much about the night before?"

"I remember an incident around that time which you did not find amusing but I did," I said. "You had given a concert in Los Angeles to the usual crowded house, and we learned that Charlie Chaplin and Douglas Fairbanks [Fairbanks senior, of course] were in the audience. After your final encore you went to the artists' room to change your shirt, and you commanded the man who guarded your door to let no one in until you gave him the signal. You had almost changed, and were about to give the man the signal to open the door to your friends and to the usual horde of signature hunters, when we heard a mighty roar like the advance of an army in the corridor. 'You can open the door now,' you called out to the guard, hastily adjusting your tie. The man flung open the door, and we saw hundreds of people rush past it and on toward the rear entrance of the hall. It turned out that the stampede had been caused by the exit of Chaplin and Fairbanks, whom your audience had rushed out to see. You had been overlooked, for once."

"And you know," Jascha said laughing, "I would have liked to join the crowd, I was so movie-struck myself in those days."

"You certainly were," I agreed, "and so was your mother. Once you nearly lost one of your recitals because of your and your mother's fondness for the movies. You had a concert in an Indiana town, I forget which, and we had two hours in Chicago before our train left. You suggested that we go to a movie house where Constance Talmadge—remember her? She was a popular movie star—was appearing in a romantic comedy. We went, you, your mother, your father, your manager and myself. An hour and a quarter later the manager signaled us to leave for the station. You and your mother asked for another quarter of an hour, the picture was too exciting to leave just then. Fifteen minutes later the manager signaled us again. But Miss Talmadge was more romantically involved than ever, and you and your mother flatly refused to budge. The manager's plea that we'd miss the only train that would get us to the concert in time failed to impress either of you. So the manager ran out, hired a limousine, rushed to the station to retrieve our luggage, where we had checked it, and rushed back to the movie house. It was only when Miss Talmadge had cleared up the misunderstanding with her screen lover and was proceeding with him arm in arm toward the sunset that you and your mother willingly left the theatre. Our train had gone long before. We got into the limousine and drove at a perilous clip for hours, arriving in the Indiana town only just in time to dress and rush to the concert hall."

"There were so many hairbreadth incidents that I had forgotten this one," Jascha said. "My poor manager must

25

have had a difficult time with me. How often did he have to use what influence he could get to delay the departure of trains a few minutes! In those days I never seemed to be able to be on time, either for trains or for concerts—and it never occurred to me to practice the violin. And now I'm going to confess something. There came a time when my disinclination to practice caught up with me. After a certain New York recital, W. J. Henderson, the music critic of the *Sun*, hinted in his review that I was letting the public—and him—down, and that I had better watch my step. Though it was hard to bear, the warning came in the nick of time. I began to take a good look at myself. I started to practice seriously. I curbed my youthful extravagances. I shall always be grateful to Henderson. He jolted me out of my complacency and put me on the right path. Critics *can* sometimes be very helpful."

Not long after Henderson's constructive reproof, Heifetz was playing better than ever. Arturo Toscanini, who in his long life had heard great violinists like Wieniawski, Joachim, Ysaye and Sarasate, declared that Heifetz was the finest of all string players. After a performance by Heifetz of the Brahms *Concerto* with the Philharmonic, Toscanini conducting, the Maestro said that he had never heard the *Concerto* so exquisitely played. The conductor and violinist became great friends. And one day when Toscanini was visiting Heifetz in the latter's ample but unpretentious farmhouse in Connecticut, he said something that obliquely revealed his reverence for the violinist's art. I had asked him how he liked Heifetz's pre-Revolutionary frame house. "Oh," he replied, "a man like Heifetz should have a grander place, one more befitting his stature as an artist. His apartment in New York suits him better." (This apartment was, actually, one of Heifetz's youthful follies. It was situated on the top floor of a large office building on Park Avenue, the only residential quarters in that structure. The living room was nearly sixty feet in length, and someone once remarked that Heifetz should supply his visitors with roller skates. I remember a charity concert given in it by Heifetz and Horowitz before an audience of several hundred. There were also great parties and amateur theatricals made memorable by Heifetz's thespian talents and the charm and affability of his first wife, the beautiful Florence Vidor.)

Musical artists are notoriously disinclined to withdraw from public life, a weakness that has often resulted in disastrous yearly "farewell" tours. Heifetz seems to have been spared this failing. Having reached his sixties (he has two sons, a daughter and two grandchildren), he embarked on a realistic program to curtail his public appearances, and he expects in the course of time to "cease upon the midnight" hour with his musical faculties fairly intact. As an illustration of what he wants to avoid, he cites the case of a certain artist he was invited to hear in London some years ago. A very old man carrying a cello came out on the stage, and when he began to play his arm trembled so that he could scarcely keep the bow on the strings. Heifetz was puzzled and embarrassed by the pathetic display. His host, however, said cheerfully, "Ah, but you should have heard him twenty-five years ago!"

"The English are so very loyal," Jascha comments as he rises to fix me another drink. "Americans are not so sentimental. They expect an artist to be up to snuff at all times," he adds.

"Well, you have nothing to worry about," I tell him.

"Having heard you play the Mozart *D Major Concerto* a few days ago in San Francisco, as well as the illustrations you offered your students this morning, I would say you are in top form."

Jascha brings me my drink. "I hope that's true, not only for the sake of the public but also for the sake of my pupils, for I should like to pass on what I know to them. I am beginning to understand why artists like Liszt, Joachim and Auer devoted so much of their time to teaching. To be an artist is like being entrusted with something precious for a brief time. It is an artist's duty to hand it on, like those Greek runners who passed on the lighted torch, one to another. Also, I find teaching, much to my surprise, a pleasure. By the way, did you notice how well she played the Chausson *Poème?*"

VLADIMIR HOROWITZ

ONE EVENING RECENTLY I went to interview the pianist Vladimir Horowitz at his house on East Ninety-fourth Street in New York City. My wife came with me, for we have been friends of Wanda and "Volodya" Horowitz for many years.

When we arrived the pianist answered the doorbell. He greeted us warmly and kissed my wife's hand. Despite his thirty-one years in America, Horowitz clings to his Old World manners, such as kissing ladies' hands and accompanying his visitors to the front door when they leave.

My wife glanced down the corridor in search of our hostess.

"Wanda is not home," Horowitz said apologetically in his high-pitched voice.

"Not home?" my wife repeated in dismay.

"Not home," Horowitz iterated rather shamefacedly.

My wife thought it odd. "But she told me she'd be here," she said testily. "We were to play canasta."

"She's not home," Horowitz said again, shaking his head sadly. "I doesn't know where she went, or when she cames back. *Ach! Bozhe moi!*" He sighed heavily, like some distressed person in a Russian novel. "But please," he continued, brightening, "permit me to show you our new

31

kitchen and dining room. Wanda makes them over completely, yes. The cost is *terrible*. But everything is new, everything."

He led us into the kitchen and showed us the new stainless-steel sinks, cabinets, closets, the dishwasher, laundry machine and other innovations which had gone to make the cost "terrible." He was proud of his dining room, the ceiling of which had been newly frescoed by a well-known painter.

To smooth over our host's obvious unhappiness about the strange absence of his wife, I recalled a party I had once attended a long time ago, at this very house, when it was owned by the late playwright George Kaufman. I described to my host one of the "turns" I particularly remembered, a song-and-dance number executed by Kaufman's colleague Robert E. Sherwood, who, flourishing a straw hat and a cane, enchanted the guests with a solemn, almost funereal rendition of *When the Red, Red Robin Comes Bob-Bob-Bobbin' Along*, at the end of which the tall, lanky dramatist went into a soft-shoe maneuver and exited with an "off-to-Buffalo" shuffle.

Horowitz listened raptly. He is fond of amateur theatricals, and is himself an amateur actor of ability. I reminded him of a party at which he had assumed the character of a befuddled but determined aspirant for a scholarship at a fictional music school. Clad in a skin-tight checked suit, his neck encased in a long woolen muffler, his hair slicked down and parted in the middle, he looked and spoke and acted like a member of the Moscow Art Theater. "I play the piano" was the only line allotted him, and he kept repeating it desperately in answer to the many questions put to him by the supposed head of the supposed school. He smiled with satisfaction at my recollection of his performance. "I enjoy acting very much," he said.

32

Horowitz now led us upstairs; and there in the living room stood Wanda Horowitz waiting to receive us. It was another thespian triumph for the pianist, and he laughed with childish glee at the way he had taken us in. Though fully aware of his boyish delight in playing practical jokes, we had been completely fooled by the realism of his deception. When his wife saw our surprise and learned of her husband's bit of play-acting, her comment was an indulgent, affectionate. *"Stupido!"*

Wanda Horowitz's close connection to musical greatness brings to mind the identification of a certain great Elizabethan lady—"Sidney's sister, Pembroke's mother"; in Wanda's case, this might be paraphrased to "Horowitz's wife, Toscanini's daughter." It is hardly possible for any woman to be musically better related. In voice and looks Wanda Horowitz is startlingly like her famous father. At the same party where her husband was so effective as a simpleton student, Wanda, in male attire, took off her father to the life. And Toscanini, who was present, laughed immoderately at his daughter's brilliant impersonation of himself. In addition, Wanda Horowitz is a musical artist in her own right. Unknown to her father, who disapproved of more than one musician in his family, she had studied voice for some years. Wanda once sang *"Ah, fors' è lui"* from *La Traviata* for me. It was a fine, professional performance, and I congratulated her. "But please," she begged, "don't tell Father. He would be very angry if he knew I studied singing."

At one end of the Horowitzes' living room two concert grands stand side by side. Horowitz teaches piano to a few gifted students, and when they play a concerto he plays the orchestral part on the second piano. I was once present at such a performance and I couldn't help feeling sorry for the soloist. Though the student was first-rate, it seemed to me that the teacher at the second piano stole the show—of course, quite unwittingly. Small wonder that he did. Vladimir Horowitz is one of the great pianists, equally gifted as musician, technician and interpreter.

On the pianos stand framed photographs of Horowitz's favorite musicians, all warmly inscribed to him—Toscanini, Rachmaninoff, Paderewski, Rubinstein, Milstein, Heifetz, Hofmann. On the walls hang four masterpieces of painting. One is a portrait of Madame Manet by her husband, Édouard Manet. ("When you write about this picture," Horowitz said earnestly, "please makes the spelling correct; don't put an 'o' instead of an 'a.' There is great difference between Manet and Monet, ah, yes!") The other paintings are a pastel by Degas of jockeys on their mounts, a head of a girl by Rouault and, perhaps the cream of the collection, Picasso's *Acrobat en Repos*. The Picasso is an unusually large canvas. The young acrobat has classic features. He is seated, waiting, with knees crossed and arms folded, the entire figure and the expression of the face conveying youthful power and a kind of sophisticated and, at the same time, innocent assurance.

Horowitz, belying his fifty-eight years, now threw himself gracefully on a sofa immediately underneath the Picasso and reclined at ease. His face is youthful-seeming, long and narrow, his brow furrowed, his nose significant, his eyes expressive, shrewd and intelligent. He wore a brown suit, a colorful vest and a bow tie. There appeared to be an affinity between him and the acrobat in the picture. Each radiated charm and security in the practice of his art. Mastery was implicit in the latent strength and nimbleness of the painted figure, in the bold innocence of its face; it was implicit also

34

in the pianist's confident, graceful disposal of himself on the couch, and excitingly confirmed when, a few moments later, he leaped up, went to one of the pianos and played some pages of Scriabin to illustrate a point he was making. The acrobat had only to rise and step out of his frame, and one was certain he would go into his routine as easily and as beautifully as the pianist had played. Each gave one the assurance of being in the presence of the ultimate virtuoso.

Horowitz returned to his sofa. But now he seemed troubled about something. There was a pained expression around his eyes, and he knit his brows as he leaned forward and put a question to me. "Tell me," he asked anxiously, "was it *your* idea to write a piece about me?"

I assured him the idea was not mine, and he smiled with relief, as if he were some obscure student of the piano hoping for a career but disinclined to be beholden to a friend for its furtherance. He relaxed under the Picasso and murmured, "I am glad it wasn't *your* idea. Now, what must I tell you?"

"Oh, everything," I said.

"That would be too much," he replied, laughing. His laugh, like his voice, is high-pitched, and has a personal quality, as if what causes it concerns himself only.

"But I shall begin," he announced innocently. Then a thought struck him and he chuckled. "You know, the funny thing is that I did not want to be pianist at all! I became pianist by accident."

"How do you mean, by accident?"

"Believe me, by accident." His face lit up with an expression of secret cleverness at having hoaxed the entire musical world. "Yes, I wanted to be composer, not pianist. Of course it is good for composer to play piano a little; so my mother, who was good pianist herself, she teach me to play piano a little when I am child, maybe four years old. When I am eleven I was admitted to Conservatory in Kiev—you know Kiev is place I am born. And soon they say I am most tal*ent*, I am not ashamed to tell you this, because everybody say so, even Scriabin, and I have no idea to be pianist, only composer. Scriabin, who was friend of family, was very clever man, because he tells to my mother, 'Your son will always be good pianist, but that is not enough, no. He must be cultured man also.' So my mother send me to school and gymnasium—gymnasium is Russian high school, but they teach more, oh, much more than in American high school— and she give me to read many books, all good books in the world. In music she play four hands on the piano with me, symphonies, operas, chamber music, everything. As a hoping composer (funny, no?) I was curious to learn what has been composed from the beginning time in music. So when I am still young I learns repertoire of all instruments and can play opera, Italian, French, German, Russian from memory. That is not so today, is it? Today peoples know music of their own instrument, but nothing else. That is not good, I think."

I asked Horowitz if his friendship with Sergei Rachmaninoff dated from Russia. He said he met Rachmaninoff in America but that he first heard him play in Russia.

Wanda Horowitz, at a card table a few feet from us, now interposed. "Tell him, Volodya, how you first heard Rachmaninoff in concert." Horowitz laughed like a child.

"Ah, yes," he said. "It was such a funny thing that I must tell you. The concert was sold out and I had no ticket. So I went to hall. I walk behind a very tall man. I am small child, you know. And the tall man, when he went into concert, I walk between his legs into hall and nobody see me." He went off into gales of laughter.

"You know," he resumed, after he had laughed himself out, "my father was not timid man, my father, not at all. Through friend he begged Rachmaninoff to hear me play. And Rachmaninoff, who *was* timid man himself, was afraid to say no, and made appointment for me and my mother at hotel. But when we arrived there they tells us he already leave Kiev by train! Many years later, in America, I asked him why he ran away from me, and he tells to me because he hate children prodigies, and he was worried that if I was no good he would have to lie to my mother and tell her I was good, which would be no good, yes?"

(It is nearly impossible to convey in words Horowitz's charming Russian accent, his pleasant disregard of contemporary pronunciation, and his blithe indifference to English grammar, such as his general avoidance of the article, both definite and indefinite, his substitution of the singular for the plural and vice versa, and many other delightful linguistic oddities.)

After the anecdote about his failure to play for Rachmaninoff, Horowitz settled back comfortably on his sofa and said nothing further, as if the interview was over. I said, "Please continue"; and sitting up in surprise he exclaimed, "Oh, you want some more? *Wand*otchka, he wants more!"

"Well," his wife said quietly, laying down a large number of cards face up, "give him more." Horowitz shrugged his shoulders wonderingly, reclined anew and went on with his story.

"I had a wonderful teacher in composition and piano at Kiev Conservatory, in name Blumenfeld. Blumenfeld was pupil of Tchaikovsky and friend to Anton Rubinstein and

37

everybody the best musicians of Europe. When I am sixteen Blumenfeld said I must to graduate. For my graduation I plays long program on the piano before the whole pupils and twenty-five professors who sit at long table under my nose, can you imagine? But I am not nervous, piano is not difficult for me. I finish with Liszt *Don Juan Fantasy*, difficult piece, and then all the peoples and the twenty-five professors stand up and makes me ovation. Everybody say I must to give recital before publicum right away. So I give two recitals in Kiev, and both houses full. I am glad. Not, believe me, because of success; but because my father, who engineer was, lose all his moneys in Revolution, and I can now give him my moneys. The Ukraine was every day attack by foreign army, and when I play I could hear noise of guns and bombs in street. Terrible! But I had success, and my father tooks me to Leningrad to make debut with Persymfans. Persymfans is Russian abbreviations for orchestra without conductor. Persymfans very *che*lebra orchestra at that time, very."

He smiled in recalling that important event. "It comes to my head" (Horowitz often thinks in French and translates literally into English), "it comes to my head how I got that engagement. My father, he went to Persymfans' concertmeister, Zeitlin whose name was, and he tells to him, 'My son Vladimir is excellent pianist, believe me. Please do me the pleasure to let him play Rachmaninoff *Number Three* with your orchestra.' My father speak in such a way that Zeitlin think it was something good, and he say 'Yes'; so I play Rachmaninoff *Number Three* with Persymfans and have big success; and I gives that winter twenty-three recitals, imagine, in Leningrad. And, funny! many young girls offer to clean concert hall for privilege to hearing my concerts; they are poor, no? and they like my playing so much. I makes lots money to give to my father and to pay for my debuts in Berlin, London and Paris. It cost much moneys to make debuts in those places. I have no more to tell you," he finished abruptly.

Wanda spoke up with another suggestion. "You forgot to tell him about Milstein," she said over her shoulder.

"Oh, yes," her husband exclaimed, "excuse me. It happened in Kiev, before I go to Leningrad. Milstein cames in Kiev for a concert, and has some tea at my house, and ask me to play. So what do I play for Milstein? You think perhaps I play Beethoven, Chopin, Rachmaninoff? Oh, no! Not at all. I plays to Milstein symphonies and operas, and then I plays with him all sonatas and concertos for violin. Can you imagine how surprised Milstein? He cames to tea and stay five years in Kiev because me. We play together music for violin and piano always. Funny?"

"Tell him," said Wanda again, "about the man who examined your passport when you left Russia." Horowitz sighed, a tender expression suffusing his face as he remembered. "Ah, yes," he said, "it is so. They permits me to leave Russia in 1925."

"They let you leave, just like that?"

"Yes," he said, "they permits me to leave for the purpose of study. That is the reason I explain to them. At the border I am nervous and white. I think they stop me. In this moment my heart I don't know where it was." He heaved another sigh. "And you know a funny thing? The soldier who tooks my passaport he look at me. Then he say, 'Do not please forget your motherland.' I was very touching."

At this emotional point Wanda suggested a break. She brought in coffee, cheese, biscuits and a tray of pastries. Horowitz, who is abstemious, touched nothing, but urged me to try the pastries which, he said, he had himself bought in a "backery" on Madison Avenue during his afternoon walk. I sipped my coffee and gazed with envy at the master-pieces of painting on the walls. I marveled aloud at the pianist's canny judgment in their selection.

"Oh, nobody tell me what to buy," he said with pride. "I study books about history of painting. I go to all museums. Then I buy what I like. I can please only myself in thing like picture, no? The Picasso I buy for nothing, eighteen thousand dollar. And the other day, believe me, I gives my word to you, somebody offer me two hundred thousand dollar for Picasso. He had check ready, right here. People want for me to sell to them also Degas; beautiful picture Degas, you think? Rouault and Manet too. I loves Manet. The picture is his wife, you know. You cannot see her face because hat cover it, but the green leaves, the vitality of the nature is there wonderfully. But while we have bread to eat I don't sell them, eh, Wandotchka?" He looked question-ingly at his wife, who, without turning around, nodded assent.

"And you know a funny thing," he pursued, "Heifetz he telephone me one day in middle of afternoon from Cali-fornia, imagine! And he ask what pictures he must buy. Of course I have only one thing to tell to him. I tell him, 'Jascha, buy only the best.' Yes, I think, I am right in so telling him."

Horowitz's consuming passion for the best in art often threatened to make serious inroads on his finances. One of his recent temptations was another Manet which he grew to admire inordinately after several visits to a New York art gallery. Soon he felt he could not live without the second Manet; and at last, unable to stand it longer, he probed his financial situation and recklessly made the dealer a substantial offer. The dealer turned it down. His desire to own the picture now at fever heat, the pianist raised his offer. The dealer remained adamant. And Horowitz arrived home in a state of dejection.

Desiring to cheer her husband up, if only for that evening, Wanda Horowitz telephoned me, told me the story of his involvement with the Manet, and proposed that I telephone Horowitz, assume the voice of the exasperating dealer, and offer to come down in price, yet still not to the point which Horowitz could afford. I was afraid Horowitz would recognize my voice, but Wanda assured me he would be too excited to suspect a hoax. Then she briefed me on the dealer's intonation and his use of English.

I telephoned Horowitz, and I could hear him gasp when I said, "Mr. Horowitz, this is ———— speaking." I told him I had thought the matter over and had decided that for a great artist like him I was now willing to reduce the price for the Manet. I had hardly finished when Horowitz broke in, his voice quivering with excitement, "Believe me, it isn't I think your price is too much. No. But I begs you to understand that musicians, even the best, are not millionaires. Yes, is true I play many concert, but the Government he takes much moneys from us artists, and not much is left for us. Please, if I am rich man like Mellon, like Rockefeller, I give you more for picture than you ask from me. But, please, I am not Rockefeller. *Only* Horowitz!"

His voice rose in pitch and intensity as he spoke. I was so touched by his ardor that I could hardly resist unmasking myself. However, it was the kind of histrionic deception that Horowitz would himself enjoy playing, and I stifled my emotion and said, "I am sorry, Mr. Horowitz, but that is

41

the very best I can do," and hung up. Wanda had been listening in on the extension phone in her room. Now Horowitz rushed in to tell her the great news. "Maybe next time he telephone the price will be so I can buy," he told her breathlessly. Needless to say the dealer did not telephone again; and when Horowitz next saw him, denied ever having called. Both pianist and dealer were mystified; and will remain so, unless they happen to read this article.

The coffee-break over, the ladies returned to canasta; and Horowitz, at my prodding, resumed the recital of his history.

"It is 1926, and Arthur Judson, the manager, hear me in Paris and gives me contract for America. I come to New York in 1928 and make debut with Philharmonic. I play Tchaikovsky concerto and make success. I plays many concerts in all United States. And, you know, from beginning I takes my playing very seriously. Believe me, I am terrifying about responsibility to public. Some artists go to hall only at time of concert. I, no. I go to hall in afternoon. I see if piano is good, is tun-ed, plac-ed. I practice in hall one, two, maybe three hour. I eats nothing. I cannot play with big stomach. After concert I eat, yes.

"And I always refuse to play outdoor," he continued. "Why? Because bad acoustic. Only exception is Hollywood Bowl, where acoustic are good, is not so, Wandotchka? I sound good in Bowl, I think. I am not boosting. I simple tell truth. I never accept to play in television or cinema. They offer me lots money, but I say no, because to play well it must be in good hall or in good studio for records. So, funny, I lose more moneys than I make. Is true. Ask Wanda. Yes, I am terrifying about responsibility.

"When I came to America I am very happy. I am young man, *absolutely* twenty-five. I make the success and the lots of money. I buy large Studebaker and hire chauffeur. Then, sad, come crash. I lose lots money, maybe seventy pret*sent*. But in few years I make moneys again and I buy Roll'-Royce. Imagine!"

In 1933 Horowitz played Beethoven's *Emperor Concerto* with Toscanini and the Philharmonic; and at a supper party after the concert he met Wanda Toscanini. Horowitz, still under the spell of the personality and musicianship of the great Maestro, hovered about him, and even played Chopin mazurkas on his host's piano, pointing out to Toscanini the beautiful, original harmonies and modulations, so eager was he to please him and engage his interest. Toscanini, who had been tremendously impressed with the pianist's performance of the Beethoven, listened intently to the mazurkas and smiled indulgently, as if the compositions were quite new to him. Before the evening was over Wanda Toscanini and Horowitz were sitting alone, deep in conversation; and the following day he sent her a photograph of himself with the succinct inscription: "To You." They were married some months later in Milan, Toscanini and his wife cabling their American friends news of the event "with joy."

Toscanini still exercises a potent influence on Horowitz the artist. "He was like priest in music," Horowitz said. "He was like flame. He had true, natural rhythm, so seldom even in good musicians. Most artists, they imitate rhythm. It comes not from the inside. But with Toscanini everything comes from the inside. He was genius, but he never stopped studying. He ask much from everybody. But he asked much more from himself. I learn many things from him. Most of all I learn from him not to be satisfied. I am never satisfied in music. I learn, learn, learn, always, always.

"And Rachmaninoff, too, was influence and friend. In

43

1942 something wonderful happen. I plays Rachmaninoff *Concerto Number Three* at symphony concert and he came and sits in last row so nobody see him, he is so modest. Then when I finish concerto he get up, walk on the stage, tooks my hand and bow with me. Everybody in hall stand up. I think it was greatest moment of my life."

I said rather impertinently, "Everybody knows you as an artist, Volodya, but they don't know what kind of man you really are. What kind of man are you? Are you easily flattered? Can you take criticism?"

He laughed uneasily and pointed to his wife. "I cannot tell," he said ruefully. "You must say him, Wanda."

Wanda paused in her game and said earnestly, "Volodya is not easily flattered. And he is not at all opinionated. He listens. Yes, he can take criticism. Once he played a Schubert sonata, and after the concert I said to him, 'You played too slow. I thought it never would finish.' And Volodya thought it over and said, 'You may be right. It is the first time I play the sonata. I am not sure myself about the tempo.' And, you know, the next time he played the Schubert it took five minutes less."

Although he continues to make records, Horowitz has not played in public for some years. "I take what you call sabbatical," he explained. "Believe me, before that I am playing steadily for thirty-two years in public. So I think I deserves rest and some time to read and study." And, indeed, Horowitz has read and studied extraordinarily much during his "sabbatical." There is hardly a book on music, ancient and modern, he hasn't purchased and read thoroughly. In effect, he has paused in his career to review his musical knowledge and his approach to music, has thought much, and arrived at interpretive conclusions that represent a new phase in his relation to his art, and not alone to music for the piano. He has arrived at a point which very few virtuoso performers ever achieve, or want to achieve. He has, through study and contemplation, come to believe in the absolute supremacy of the composer, the same belief that was the foundation of the art of his great father-in-law. He has dedicated himself to carry out the aim and intent of the great composers, old and new, with all the resources at his command. Sometimes, as in his arrangement of a Liszt rhapsody, he adds these resources to those of the old master, whose once formidable pianistic demands are now child's play for Horowitz. But these transformations are reverently undertaken with the sole idea of having them sound as Liszt would have them sound were he alive today.

Horowitz's feeling for the music of the greatest masters is now broad and deep. In preparation for recording two Beethoven sonatas he made exhaustive researches in the history and the interpretive fate of both works. He bought and carefully examined every available printed edition of the *Appassionata* and obtained a facsimile of the original manuscript. And in Beethoven's own handwriting he found one single note that had been altered in every edition. The change of a single note in so vast a sonata as the *Appassionata* might be considered negligible. But, like the Biblical importance of the fall of a single sparrow, the substitution of a note in Beethoven can mar the characteristic physiognomy of that composer. In the *Appassionata*, the seemingly innocent change of Beethoven's clearly indicated A flat to F at the end of the last movement must be disturbing to the acute and knowledgeable listener.

During his "sabbatical" Horowitz also sought out old and rare recordings of famous singers of the past and found in them displays of beautiful phrasing, of tonal shades and musical understanding that should, but only rarely do, inform interpretive art. Chief among these mementos of a bygone age are the records of the great Italian baritone Mattia Battistini, of which Horowitz has, I believe, a complete collection. "And do you know Allesandro Bonci's record of *Spirto Gentil* from Donizetti's *La Favorita?*" he asked eagerly. "Wanda, please get record and play for him *Spirto Gentil.*"

Wanda rose to fetch the record. "We played it for Father," she said, "only a few months before he died. He was deeply moved."

We listened to Bonci's *Spirto Gentil.*

"Who can sing like that today?" Wanda Horowitz demanded.

It was now quite late and time to go. "Oh, no, please," Horowitz pleaded. "Now is best part of evening. We talks now about music, not about me. I do not care to go to cinema, not to theater. I prefers to sit and talk to friends about music, like this."

"The other night," I said, sinking back in my chair, "we were listening to the radio. A pianist was playing music that sounded familiar, but I was unable to identify the piece. It was very much like something of Beethoven's, but I couldn't be sure."

Horowitz jumped from his sofa. "Yes, yes," he exclaimed, "Wanda and I heard it too. It was my record of Clementi *G Minor Sonata,* and you are right; it is so much like Beethoven that Beethoven could have composed it. Fantastic what Beethoven owe to Clementi." And Horowitz launched into a charmingly worded analysis of Beethoven's indebtedness to his Italian forerunner and contemporary.

46

Half an hour later Horowitz was on the subject of Tchaikovsky, whom he adores. "What a great man, Tchaikovsky! Rachmaninoff realize Tchaikovsky well. He says to me many times, 'Tchaikovsky is greatest Russian composer. He has enough melody for hundreds composers.' I meet friend the other day, and he say to me, '*Pique Dame* is not so good opera.' 'Not so good opera?' I say to him. '*Pique Dame* is *best* Tchaikovsky opera.' I ask him, 'You know *Pique Dame?*' He says, 'No.' 'Then why you speak so?' I tells him."

Horowitz asked me if I knew the opera *Mazeppa* by Tchaikovsky, and I confessed I did not. "No?" he cried, anticipating his own pleasure in acquainting me with this little-known work. "Wandotchka, please play record of *Mazeppa.*"

We heard parts of *Mazeppa.* Horowitz, who knows every note of the opera, exhibited the eagerness and enthusiasm of a child, calling my attention to felicities of orchestration and forceful dramatic moments. He listened lying stretched out on his sofa, suddenly sitting up, leaning forward, tying himself into a knot, his keen eyes glued to the phonograph and often shifting to me, seeking in my eyes recognition of the power or beauty of a passage.

"Wonderful, *Mazeppa*, no?" he cried ecstatically at the end. "But Rimsky-Korsakoff is beautiful too, ah, very beautiful. You know *Sadko*, the opera Rimsky-Korsakoff? Wanda, please play record *Sadko.*"

It was really very late now, and I asked Horowitz if he was tired.

"Tired!" he exclaimed, scorning the idea. "Never!"

"Then," I said, "if you are not tired, why don't you play for us? I hear that you have made your own arrangement

47

of Liszt's *Nineteenth Rhapsody*. I don't know it and I am eager to hear your arrangement of it."

He was apologetic as he went to the piano. "You know, when I am making arrangement I don't practice," he said. "So you must please excuse playing. *Nineteenth Rhapsody* is difficult in my arrangement. You shall hear. But first, please, I must ask you if you know Liszt's *Nuages Grises*. It very small piece Liszt compose the year he die. Listen and tell me who compose it. You will not know."

He played *Nuages Grises*, and I had to admit it was quite unlike Liszt, anticipating as it did the impressionism of Debussy and Ravel. Horowitz laughed with satisfaction, then prepared to play his arrangement of the *Nineteenth Rhapsody*. Presently the room resounded with majestic harmonies. Horowitz commented as he played: "This part, Liszt. This part, me. Here I strengthen. Here I makes a little different. Liszt, you know, was old man now and weak. Sometime he imitate himself. But now, listen. Now comes *friska*." (*Friska* is the fast part of a Hungarian dance.)

At the *friska* Horowitz's hands began at first softly, then they gradually brought up the volume and flew over the entire keyboard with reckless abandon, but deadly accuracy, whipping up a whirlwind of orgiastic patterns, reaching ever greater, more powerful climaxes, and finishing off with a dazzling flurry of multitudinous notes, cruelly intricate, and huge flying chords of steely power and magnificence. The effect was overpowering, the more so because of the violent contrast between the pianist's soft, caressing tone at the beginning and the grandiose power he loosed at the end. Yet it was more than a thrilling display of virtuosity. It was the controlled playing of a formidably gifted artist at the height of his mental, musical and physical powers, when all

48

the facets of his art are so fused that one is aware only of the totality of the impression.

"You must excuse playing," Horowitz pleaded again, as he accompanied us to the front door. "When I practice a little more it will go much better. And when you comes next time we play record of *Sadko*. The record was made in Russia twelve years ago. It is very beautiful, you will hear . . ."

"My dear Volodya," I broke in, "I don't care anything about *Sadko* at the moment. I am still under the spell of your playing. What a pity the public cannot hear you play as we did tonight."

"Oh," Horowitz said as we shook hands, "the public will soon hear. I make record of the *Rhapsody*."

"That's fine," I said, "but you must also play to people in concert halls." Horowitz knitted his brows and murmured, "You think so? Wandotchka," he called to his wife, who was putting things to rights in the hall upstairs, "he thinks I must play to public in concerts." His wife called down that she quite agreed. Horowitz opened the front door, and an icy blast swept through the entrance.

"One day soon," he said, "maybe I plays."

From upstairs came Wanda Horowitz's warning voice. "Volodya, you will catch cold."

Horowitz kissed my wife's hand and reluctantly shut the door.

GIAN CARLO MENOTTI

"WHEN YOU OPEN MY BODY," said Mary Tudor on her deathbed, "you will find Calais written on my heart." Mary had lost Calais to the French. Substitute Spoleto for Calais and you will have an idea of the feeling composer Gian Carlo Menotti has had these past five years for the beautiful Italian hill town. Unlike Mary Tudor, Menotti has not lost a town but rediscovered one, and made it the scene of his *Festival of Two Worlds*. Also, unlike the English Queen who wanted Calais for political and economic reasons, Menotti, as the foremost operatic composer of our times, has no such mundane reasons for running a musical festival. But, since there must be a reason for everything, I tried to discover what it was that made him undertake so taxing and time-consuming a venture in a hitherto unobtrusive and little-known city in a remote part of Italy.

I arrived in Spoleto on the second morning of last summer's *Festival of Two Worlds*, and called at the Palazzo Campello, a vast, rather shabby building where Menotti lives, gives parties and conducts festival business. I found him talking on the telephone. He looked disheveled and quite distressed. *"Mi dispiace molto,"* he kept repeating, *"molto, molto, molto."* He put the receiver down with a gesture of frustration, greeted me hastily and gave vent to his displeasure with the situation in Spoleto.

"The Italians are so slow getting anything done. It is hard for me to take. I am so used to the snap, the dispatch with which things are done in America. The Italians are a charming people—am I not an Italian myself? But they are slow, happy-go-lucky (I was probably like that once, before I came to America). And they are disarming. It's not easy to bawl them out. One feels like such a pig, and they look at you with such hurt eyes that you are moved to tears and want to embrace them and apologize for your mistrust and rudeness. Still, here in Spoleto, until the very last moment, nothing is ready. I'm really at my wit's end. I have to attend to every detail myself, to say nothing of having to raise the money for the festival."

"How are your finances this year?" I inquired innocently.

"Terrible!" he said.

"Why don't you chuck the whole thing? You should be writing operas instead."

"I'm often tempted to chuck it," he admitted. "But there's my compulsion to keep on doing it. The whole town depends on me, on the Festival—the shopkeepers, the restaurants, the hotels—we now have two new, up-to-date hotels in the center of town and they're full up. Then there are the scene painters, the Italian and American singers, the orchestra, the chorus, the ballet—literally hundreds of people. How can I fail them? Could I live with myself if I did? I know you think if I gave the whole thing up it would benefit my music. But I don't believe it would. I can't see myself sitting down to compose operas if I knew I was taking the bread out of the mouths of the poor people of Spoleto and the students and musicians I have managed to assemble here."

"The Spoletini got along without you for hundreds of years," I couldn't help observing.

54

"Yes, but," Menotti replied, "they are by now accustomed to the summer prosperity the Festival brings them. It doesn't take long to get used to a good thing."

"Anyway," I went on, "I think it is more important for the world, and that includes the Italians, that you devote all your time to writing music."

"Of course I'm flattered that you consider my music so important," Menotti said. "But I am unable to take my music as seriously as you do. Life and people are more important to me. Spoleto is a symbol of my guilt complex."

Although it is fashionable nowadays to proclaim a guilt complex whether one has one or not, there was an earnestness, a simplicity about his confession that assured me that Menotti's guilt complex was not an invention.

"You see," he said apologetically, "I have always been a happy man. And because I have been happy I never felt that writing music was enough. It has been very difficult for me to ignore the world. I am terribly conscious of the world around me. This sense of guilt is, I think, a witness to my character. To satisfy my desire of feeling useful I waste my time in a sort of—a sort of unending, useless kindness. If I weren't a composer I probably would be a nurse in a hospital. This conflict in my life is tremendously strong. Spoleto satisfies my craving to be useful, to help people. At the same time, I often feel as you do, that I am wasting my time. You are right, of course. I should be composing. Yet I always regret not having a family and children. I feel selfish in dedicating my life to myself. I feel well, I sleep well, I'm happy. But often I feel I am wrong. One shouldn't be happy, should one? You see, fundamentally I am dissatisfied with myself because I believe exactly the opposite of what T. S. Eliot expresses in *The Cocktail Party*. I don't believe that one can somehow find happiness or excuse in partaking of

55

the things of the world. I feel that the fact that martyrs exist in the world is an indictment of anyone who is happy. To put it more bluntly, I feel that happiness is a form of cowardice."

A tall young servant in a white jacket came in. "Oh, Alfredo," Menotti said, and there was honey in his voice, "I've invited the cast of *The Love of Three Oranges* to supper here tonight after their performance."

"How many, Maestro?" the tall servant asked deferentially.

"Oh, I don't really know, Alfredo. Fifty—sixty—maybe eighty."

"Yes, Maestro. At midnight?"

"Perhaps one in the morning would be safer. It takes time to remove make-up. Oh, yes. I've also invited the cast of *The American Dream*, and they won't be ready before one because the performance will only begin at midnight. So let's have drinks at twelve and supper at one, Alfredo."

"*Bene*, Maestro," the good-natured Alfredo said, beaming at Menotti, who, in turn, bestowed a charming though careworn smile on his servant. The composer's lean, lined face accentuated the worried brightness of his limpid eyes. At fifty-one Menotti still takes pains to look slim. Indeed, he reacts so sharply to physical grossness that he shuns fat people like the plague.

"You know the singer ———?" and he mentioned a member of the cast of an opera scheduled for the Festival. "When I engaged him last winter he looked quite all right. But you should see him now! He has gained at least ten pounds, gorging himself on *pasta*, and he looks like a pig. I wish you would talk to him. He might listen to you . . ."

Although Menotti looks world-weary and moves about

56

indeterminately, as if occupied with secret, tortuous things, he can summon sufficient energy for whatever he wants to do or wants done. And when all else fails he can rely on his charm. His figure and his eyes inspire sympathy, and his persuasiveness is hard to resist. But underneath his tender, worried exterior, a will and a determination reside and occasionally show themselves as implacable as they are ruthless. As a consequence, he has almost always triumphed over obstacles, and to ensure his triumphs he has used cajolery in a variety of forms and often quite shamelessly, as in his frequent "raw" appeals to the inherent sentimentality or conceit of artists whose co-operation he desires, of wealthy persons whose donations make the Festival possible, of singers who will be induced to take less than their usual fees, and even of servants who may be flattered into regarding long hours as a privilege and a contribution to patriotism and art.

In return Menotti dispenses warmth and tenderness, intimacy and, when he is flush, a generosity of such proportions as to have kept him, notwithstanding the large sums of money he earns, a poor man. He is a St. Francis among musicians, distributing his wealth to the needy, or to some cause close to his heart, like the Spoleto Festival. And when his own resources are depleted he remorselessly extracts money from the rich to give to the poor. Children are his special concern; both in Italy and in America his benefactions to the young are quite out of proportion to his means. On the other hand, Menotti is a confessed hedonist. In this he also resembles his favorite saint, but it is the young, rich, pleasure-loving Francis before he renounced the world. It is, I suspect, Menotti's inability or reluctance to cast aside the hedonism of the youthful Francis that is at the core of his guilt complex. The struggle with what he calls his baser self goes on and may never be resolved. In the meantime he salves his conscience with private charities and public atonements like the *Festival of Two Worlds*. And in the process his music lags behind.

Menotti remains a personality of contradictions. He is at one and the same time shrewd, tender, worldly, spiritual, unworldly, sensual and self-critical. Although conservative in his own approach to music, his attitude to his colleagues' is indulgent and progressive. He will not compose in the modern cacophonous, cerebral manner, but he has understanding and sympathy for the avant-garde in music, in painting, in sculpture, in literature, indeed in every manifestation of art. Last summer he filled the lovely, hilly old streets of Spoleto with huge statues of bronze and other metals, of modern design and baffling significance. His aesthetic sense, so lucid and patrician in his own music, was not at all offended by the incongruity of a huge, bronze nude full of stomach holes challenging the fifteenth-century Gothic simplicity and serenity of Spoleto's beautiful Piazza del Duomo.

"I rather like these statues," Menotti assured me, "and so do the Spoletini and the visitors. The statues are dramatic, don't you think? And the contrast between them and the ancient city is sensational." Indeed, the huge monstrosities were generally surrounded by admiring natives and tourists. The effect is certainly "sensational," and "sensation" is an important component of Menotti's character and art. It is especially prominent in his work as stage director, on which he prides himself.

"I always felt I could do better than most stage directors," he said. "And when my opera *Amelia Goes to the Ball* was rehearsed by an Italian stage director at La Scala in Milan, I became such a nuisance with my innumerable suggestions that I was chased off the stage. After that I accepted commissions to write operas only on condition that I stage them myself."

As a stage director Menotti translates action into emotion. He creates a kind of theater in the raw—the groupings, the detail, the movements make for glaring clarity. Everything on the stage is out-size and makes an immediate impact on the audience. In his staging of Bizet's *Carmen* in Spoleto during 1962, Menotti directed the toreador to sing the second verse of his song straight at a five-year-old boy instead of at the bullfighter's more mature admirers on the stage. Don José was made to stab Carmen savagely and repeatedly in the back, not, as is usual, in the heart. And as Carmen reeled from the blows, a blind man led by a little boy emerged from the wings and, tapping with his stick, slowly zigzagged across the stage. The introduction of the blind man was, obviously, a device to symbolize the groping blindness of fate.

If you ask Menotti what he most desires in life, he will answer promptly "money." He is continually in need of money. He needs it for his festival in Spoleto, for bringing poor American students to Italy, poor Italian students to America, for sending some indigent child to a hospital for an operation or aiding a friend who may be down on his luck. It was his need of money for some such unselfish purpose that sent him to the National Broadcasting Company in 1949 to ask for a commission to compose a television opera. And it was to this that the world owes Menotti's Christmas classic, *Amahl and the Night Visitors*.

Since *Amahl* is performed hundreds of times each year in

schools, colleges, opera houses, on radio and television, Menotti calls this little work his bread-and-butter opera. Its continued success all over the world is a source of both income and musical satisfaction to its self-critical, often self-doubting creator. But even more satisfying is his remembrance of a certain rehearsal of *Amahl*, a run-through without scenery and costumes and with an upright piano for an orchestra. The only spectators, aside from the cast and the people engaged in the production, were Arturo Toscanini and Olin Downes, the then music critic of the *New York Times*. At the moment of the miracle, when the crippled Amahl offers his crutch as a gift to the Christ Child and is suddenly able to walk, Toscanini and Downes broke down and wept. Later Toscanini impulsively embraced Menotti. "Thank you, my dear," the Maestro said. "You write music from the heart, not from the head, as all the other composers unfortunately do these days."

"I wish I could say that I had a poverty-stricken childhood and that my family opposed my studying music and becoming a composer," Menotti said. "It sounds so romantic for a composer to have been poor, and to have had to fight the opposition of an inartistic family. I have to admit that my family was rich, even bourgeois. On my mother's side I had relatives full of personality and with a bias toward art. One of them was an uncle who couldn't bear living with his cold, stingy, inartistic wife. He got so angry with her that he built himself another house and filled it with *objets d'art*. To his wife's horror he gave keys to this house to all his friends. This uncle had a great influence on me. He was ultra-decadent and theatrical, and I adored the unusual things he did, such as filling his house with doves.

60

"I had, in fact, lots of uncles. To describe all of them would take seven volumes at least. I also have thirteen nephews and nieces. One of my uncles was headed for the priesthood. The day he was to be ordained, he packed up and went off to South America, which was then primitive. In South America this would-be priest founded what was the first export-import house there. Then he invited my father to join him in his business and share the profits. That's how my father made lots of money. Nevertheless, my father hated business and had no love for material things. I, myself, don't mind either of these things. The only thing I shared with my father was a love of sharpening pencils. He was crazy about pencils. We children could steal and lie and he didn't mind, but if we took one of his pencils he got really mad. I still love pencils. In Mount Kisco, in my house, my maid sharpens my pencils every day and lays them out like my shirts.

"My father returned to Italy, leaving his business in the hands of a trusted employee who regularly sent him packets of money. So actually we eight children—we were a large family—had a comfortable life. All eight were always dressed in white, so naturally we had to be changed quite often. Our life in a small village on Lake Lugano had a Russian, Turgenev-like quality. Every day in the long winter my mother taught the villagers to sing Gregorian chants. We had lots of chamber music at home, and my aunt and my mother played the classics, four-hands, on the piano. One day our priest-uncle arrived with his South American Creole mistress, who was then an old woman. She had two daughters by another man. My uncle married one of the daughters but never slept with her. This uncle, having no children of his own, adored us. And this is where he and

61

our surroundings tie up with *Amahl;* for all our relatives and their children would visit us at Christmas. There were huge dinners and many gifts. The gifts were brought by relatives dressed up as the Three Wise Kings. We had lots of snow—real northern Christmases. I have terrific memories of these. In fact, the first composition I ever wrote—I was four years old—I called *Snow.* And in *Amahl* I tried to express my wonder and joy at those awesome, colorful, naïve Christmases of my childhood.

"When I was fourteen a big change came into my life. My father died. And to make things worse, his trusted employee in South America wrote that there would be no more money for us. Before leaving for South America to find out what had happened to my father's business, my mother went to Milan to consult her friend Arturo Toscanini about what to do with me. She adored having an artist in the family, as did all my relatives, but she needed advice about me. Toscanini told her that the best thing for my musical development would be for me to go to the United States, where I wouldn't know anybody and was not likely to be coddled and spoiled as I would be at home. My mother took his advice, and we sailed for New York. We were very sad. It was Christmas, and we spent the holidays alone in a room in a hotel! Then we went to Philadelphia to the Curtis Institute of Music where I played some of my things for Scalero, an Italian composer who taught composition at Curtis. I was given a scholarship. And one rainy afternoon I saw my mother off at the Broad Street Station. Both of us wept. For the first time in my life I was left alone without family or friends. I remember my terror.

"Luckily I got to know Sam Barber, a fellow pupil at Curtis. Sam, who could speak French and Italian, was the hero of the school. In fact, he could do everything I couldn't do. He sang beautifully, played and composed. No one took *me* seriously at the school except Sam. I was a bit awed at Curtis. Everybody was a genius but me. All I had behind me were some bad marks for solfeggio at the Milan Conservatory and two little operas I wrote when I was eleven. They were very primitive.

"I must tell you frankly that I am not a facile musician. What it takes other people days to do takes me weeks. My music equipment is poor. I haven't got perfect pitch."

"They say Wagner didn't either," I interjected.

"That's hardly a consolation," Menotti replied. "It is true I began early, but I was a bad student. I was a puzzle to my teachers. I had to learn in my own way or not at all. I had to develop a private technique. I had to fashion my own instruments, my own weapons, so to speak. And I did. It's a serviceable technique, but it's not the usual equipment. I could never say with Tchaikovsky who, when asked how he composed, replied, 'I sit down.' I do sit down, but I have to get up every ten minutes. I compose fitfully. I always feel in composing that I come quickly to a point of saturation. I want to be always fresh. I get up. I eat an apple. The trouble with me is that in composing I play a dual role. I am the composer. But I am also the audience, and I want to be sure that I as the audience understand clearly what the composer intended. You can compare it with having bad breath. Everybody knows it but the fellow who has it. It is an effort to be on both sides—to breathe and smell your own breath!"

Here Alfredo came in and said, "Telephone, Maestro." Menotti took up the receiver, listened a while and exploded in Italian. "*Dio mio*," he shouted. "*Imbecile! Mi dispiace molto. Molto! Molto!*'' The agonized, despairing expression on his face reminded me of the look on the faces of the Laocoön statue in the Vatican. Menotti was struggling again in the toils of his Festival troubles. I left him sputtering into the telephone.

An hour later I watched him piloting two old ladies, obviously prospective sponsors, across the Piazza del Duomo to the tiny eighteenth-century theater. I asked him when I could see him again. He rapidly reviewed what he still had to do that day.

"I'm staging *Carmen* from three to six. Perhaps you'd like to come? Six to eight I have Festival business to attend to. How about nine? No, I am sorry. At nine I'm expected at the dress rehearsal of two American one-act plays. Would you like to come? The public performance takes place at midnight tonight, and of course I'll have to be there too. I have an idea. Why don't you come to the Palazzo at eight? We can talk while I'm dressing. I'll skip dinner. And I'll lop off an hour from my business."

I arrived at the Palazzo promptly at eight and found Menotti deep in a discussion of *Carmen* with Thomas Schippers, the conductor, and several aides. I waited around, and at last, deciding there would be no interview that evening, I made for the door. Menotti rose hastily and intercepted me. "All right, all right," he said soothingly, taking my arm. He dismissed his colleagues and ushered me into his bedroom. "Where were we?" he asked, fetching his dinner jacket from a bulky Victorian closet.

"You really have too much to do, Gian Carlo," I said reprovingly, "especially for a man who should be composing operas."

"Please bear with me," Menotti pleaded, starting to un-

64

dress. "I know my activity here is not easy to explain. It has much to do with my wanting to belong to something—to a community. I wanted to be released from the megalomania of the artist. Today, music suffers from this megalomania of the artist, because no composer is willing to accept the role of the minor artist. You know, many old artists were quite content to be minor. Modern artists are not. Take Bartók. He was an interesting minor composer." (I could almost hear the howls of anguish from the Bartókites.) "Bartók was inflated by himself and by his admirers. What distinguishes the great from the small artist is his monumental indifference to his classification and his concern with grand design. The small artist is only concerned with detail." He sighed deeply.

"All modern art is baroque," Menotti went on. "It is all rococo, it is all adornment. Modern music is interesting for detail. It may be amusing, but it still is mainly decorative, or marginal, never organic. Art used to be functional. Today the artist has no relation to life. He is left outside. He lives in limbo. He is rejected, therefore he rebels. My own family understood the danger, and they made art a part of their lives. An artistic event meant something to them. As for me, I found that music wasn't enough. That's why I am here in Spoleto. I wanted to find out if I could be part of the people here, and I found I could. We have become heroes in this little town. We are making the city live. You will ask, did it have to be Spoleto? Why not an American town? Well, I chose Italy because Europeans can't afford to come to America. Besides, I think American artists suffer from a kind of provincialism. They love to import art, but they don't export it. It's only in the last few years that America exports art because of Russia. America still doesn't recognize the propaganda effect of art. The French artist really feels he is a part of his nation, and his government uses art for the welfare of the nation, and that gives the French artist a sense of dignity. In America the artist is treated as a special case, a strange phenomenon. Artists are held to be misfits, an extra thing."

I must have looked impatient, for Menotti stopped and shook his head deprecatingly. "I see," he said, smiling at me, "you'd rather I talk about myself. Where was I about myself? Oh, yes, I remember. At the Curtis Institute of Music. Well, I developed very slowly at the school, and Sam Barber helped me a lot. For one thing, he introduced me to the music of Brahms, and I caught his enthusiasm, and like most musicians, I went through my Brahms period. And I found a second mother in Sam's mother, an angel if I ever saw one. She called me Johnny because Gian Carlo was too complicated for her. She lived in West Chester, Pennsylvania, and Sam and I visited her a lot. Actually, West Chester inspired my *The Old Maid and the Thief*. I took all the names from the people in that little town—Miss Todd, Miss Pinkerton and others. Of course the story didn't happen in West Chester. I invented it. But it *should* have happened there.

"Scalero liked Brahms also, so the German influence was dominant at his lessons. Though I admired Brahms, Schubert was more sympathetic to me, and he influenced me greatly. Schubert taught me to express myself simply. Moussorgsky was another composer who had much to do with my musical development. I believe an artist must have a paternity. He just doesn't grow out of nothing.

"My dream was to spend a winter in Vienna and get closer to the great composers who had lived there, especially to Schubert. Well, I managed to get to Vienna, where I

66

rented an apartment from a huge Czechoslovakian lady who smoked cigars and spent her days eating *pâté de foie gras* and drinking champagne. This woman was so huge and so lazy that she had a machine constructed that enabled her to shut and open her door without leaving her bed. In her room she had the most beautiful dressing table, and I was so taken with the extravagance and frivolity of this dressing table that it gave me the idea for my opera *Amelia Goes to the Ball*. It is really very curious how that dressing table set in motion my mind to write an opera. Because Scalero's indoctrination of German polyphonic music had taken only too well with me, and I had come to detest opera.

"I returned to America, and one day I played *Amelia* for Mary Zimbalist, who was then Mary Bok. She took me seriously, and the Curtis Institute of Music of which she was the founder had *Amelia* produced in Baltimore, Philadelphia and New York, with Fritz Reiner conducting. American critics liked *Amelia* and said that it brought a breath of fresh air into the operatic world. *Amelia* was done in Italy too. But for some unaccountable reason a strange hostility rose against me in my native land. I was insulted in the papers, I guess because America and not Italy had discovered me, and because I refused to join the Fascist party. They associated me with American ways, which they hated.

"And you know," Menotti mused, coming into the room and adjusting his suspenders, "in a funny way I consider *Amelia* my good-luck piece. At the same time it was my *bête noire*, my doom, because its success condemned me to write operas, whereas I really love to write instrumental music."

"After *Amelia* you wrote *The Old Maid and the Thief* and three years later *The Island God*, if I remember," I said, remembering.

"Don't speak of *The Island God*," Menotti said bitterly.

"The only way I can account for that fiasco—it was worse than a fiasco, it was a disaster—is that my old German indoctrination came to the surface again. I suffered an illusion of grandeur when I wrote it. It is the only one of my operas I withdrew. Yet, you know, it had a certain value for me. In it I tackled a subject too heroic for my kind of music. It was then I realized that the first duty of an artist is to know his limitations. My vein was not heroic. *The Island God* taught me that I was no Wagner.

"It also taught me what an effort it is to maintain the monster of success. So many American artists keep feeding this monster. Right after the failure of *The Island God* I was dropped as quickly as I had been taken up. I was despondent, and I tried to raise my spirits by writing a piano concerto. Someone on Morningside Heights must have seen and liked the concerto, for suddenly Columbia University commissioned me to write a chamber opera. That was how I came to write *The Medium*. All the same *The Medium* was turned down by the publishers I sent it to. With a budget of nothing at all we put on *The Medium*. There is an amusing story connected with this opera. The *New York Times* gave it a bad review. Then it was decided to bring *The Medium* to Broadway for a run. We needed another *Times* review after the Broadway opening, so I gave out that for Broadway I had revised the opera. As a matter of fact, all I did was to *add* one page of music. The *Times* critic came again to review *The Medium*, wrote that it was an *abridged* version, 'more compact.' It was a very favorable review about the very same opera he had heard and disliked before.

"Although I have written better and worse music, I consider *The Medium* the key work in my development as an operatic composer. It was with *The Medium* that I discovered what I could do in the lyric theater. It contains the potentialities of my style. The one problem I am interested in is being able to unfold a story in a lyrical way; and by that I mean to make the *recitativo*—the part that tells the story—part of the lyrical whole. Only Puccini has solved that problem. That is why I consider *La Bohème* the most important opera. Never to interrupt the lyrical flow and to indicate action at the same time—that is what I tried for. I am rather proud of *The Medium* because I believe it does this. 'It's good theater,' some people say, 'but there is no music.' They are wrong. It takes great effort to do what I did in *The Medium*. Verdi said, 'To write a good opera you must have the courage *not* to write.' Another element I tried to develop in my music is the evocative, to create a picture out of notes. For example, the *Prelude* of *Carmen* creates a great excitement before the curtain goes up. And another thing: contemporary subjects are important. The artist must find the poetry in contemporary life.

"When necessary I always sacrifice the libretto to the music. I cut scenes and scenes, often with bleeding heart, out of my operas. That was Wagner's tragedy. He wouldn't cut his words. A composer must not hesitate to be a surgeon and operate on himself."

Menotti looked at himself in a mirror and straightened his bow tie.

"What more can I tell you?" he asked plaintively. "My future plans? Well, I have to work a lot because I have more debts than one can imagine. I am working on an oratorio for Cincinnati called *The Bishop of Brindisi;* he was the man who organized the Children's Crusade, with such disastrous results. I owe NBC an opera [the NBC opera *Labyrinth* was televised on Sunday, March 3, 1963], and I am com-

69

posing *The Last Superman*, which the Paris Opera will produce next season, and the Metropolitan the following year. I still have two more operas I am dying to write. One will be *The Leper*, a subject which has occupied my mind for a long time. The other will be on Pythagoras. Do you mind walking with me to the theater?"

We left the Palazzo and descended to the Piazza del Duomo. I said something about the loveliness of the scene before us.

"Yes," Menotti agreed, "it's very lovely. Yet I can't help feeling sad. I feel defeated by the stupidity of people. What shocks me most about people is that hate joins more people than love does. The people who were around Gandhi, Tolstoi and other great souls hated one another. Love seemed to generate hate.

"At the same time, strange as it may seem, I've never been tired of life. Life has been terribly short, much too short. I have such a great desire to learn.

"In my oratorio the Bishop of Brindisi makes a final invocation to God. 'In spite of having caused the death of so many children in the ill-fated Crusade,' the Bishop says, 'I don't understand why I have been allowed to make such terrible mistakes in my life. I still believe in God, because everything we've been given has a purpose. We have a hand to eat with, an eye to see with, and the fact that we've been given a searching mind is enough proof to me that the answer exists and it will finally be given us. And the answer will be given to us in relation to the search we've made for it.'

"I must hurry in now," Menotti said as we came to the theater. "Did you get what you wanted?"

70

LEONTYNE PRICE

LEONTYNE PRICE SWEEPS into the room like a Winged Victory, the folds of her dress and light coat tugging backward as if breasting a high wind. In the amplitude of her colorful garments, in the inverted tub of her mauve hat, she is all flamboyance. Her light, chocolate skin and her large, deep, expressive eyes, liquid and soft, can easily afford her bizarre get-up; and her rich, creamy, Southern speaking voice seems like the ultimate endowment of her warm, brilliant, very human personality.

I ask myself if this is the same Leontyne Price I first got to know six or seven years ago, when she was quite unknown. Her basic character is the same. But her recent extraordinary successes have given her a self-confidence and a buoyancy that are new. Success has liberated a latent exuberance and permitted her to give play to a native sense of humor and an incorrigible enthusiasm for life. Although she makes no bones about appreciating and enjoying her success enormously, she is anything but the stereotype of a prima donna. Tremendous acclaim in Vienna, London, Milan and New York, rave reviews and fabulous publicity have not had the usual inflationary effect of fame and notoriety. Essentially she is the Leontyne Price I first knew, now more exuberant, released from the natural timidity and inhibitions of the artist who has yet to make her mark.

Her pleasure in stardom is naïve and most un-prima-donna-like. She embraces me and sits down rather breathlessly and looks about her approvingly. "Isn't it all wonderful—I mean what's happened to me." She seems to be implying "I'm happy (though I'm as studious and conscientious as ever) and I love you and everything and everybody."

Her speech is rapid and fluent, often torrential. And her pleasure in giving full expression to her sentiments, ideas and general optimism is so guileless that I hesitate to interrupt her, and I put in a word here and there only to keep her from straying from her fairy-tale story.

She tells me that she flew in from Rome, where she has a flat and where she adores living whenever her schedule permits, and to which she flies back tomorrow.

"But what a lovely apartment you have!" she exclaims, looking around at my ordinary flat as if for the first time, though she has been here often in her pre-prima-donna days. In her general euphoria she is really seeing it for the first time and feels obliged to voice her appreciation and please me. "It's a charming apartment," she insists, "it really is; I love it, it's so livable."

"Is it anything like your apartment in Rome?" I ask.

"No." She catches herself, anxious not to give a wrong impression. "I mean, I have just a little hole in the wall, very cute but very small; and did I tell you I have seven nuns for neighbors? Imagine! Seven Spanish nuns live next door. If I should want to whoop it up and have a few friends in, it's going to be extremely difficult next to seven nuns!"

"Well, I hope they're not going to seduce you into taking the veil. Did you ever wish to become a nun?"

74

"Oh, no."

"Not even when you were a child?"

A note of seriousness replaces her insouciance. Something, it seems, was expected of her when she was a child, and it was not her giving up the world.

"You see," she says soberly, "when I was a child I remember vividly always being sort of the local 'thing.' In those days I think even my mother thought I was a child prodigy just because I learned to play the piano at a very early age."

"Did you have a piano?"

"Yes. My mother, at a very great sacrifice (she was kind of a midwife, I think) paid on the installment plan for a piano for me, an upright. I must have been about eight or nine. I remember, too, the Christmas I got my bicycle. It was the happiest Christmas of my life. A piano *and* a bicycle! You see, in the South it's difficult because of the low wages, and I dᴏ mean the lowest, which is what my father earned. He was a sawmill worker, and while I can't quote what he made a week, I can assure you it wasn't much. The weekly income was supplemented by my mother, so the home budget benefited from the fact that both of my parents worked, you see."

"How many were you?" I asked.

"Just two of us. My brother and I. My brother was to me the handsomest, most intelligent boy or man, next to my father, I have ever known. My parents were married going on thirteen and a half or fourteen years before they had children. My father is now eighty-two years old, he is quite elderly, but you wouldn't believe it because he is so well preserved. My mother is considerably younger—my mother, I think, will be seventy years old next year. I remember very much in my childhood that specifically as far as my mother was concerned (she too had a beautiful voice —she sort of lifted it in the Methodist church choir at home; still does, as a matter of fact) she was always extremely protective about my having everything. You know, at times somebody in the house had to go without something in order for me to have a piano lesson, or to have a nicer dress for school, or something that she might not have had time to make for me herself had to be bought for me at the local store, which was called Fine Bros. & Madison, I think, in Laurel, Mississippi. It was kind of a dollar down and a dollar a week deal, you know. In those days ten dollars was an enormous amount of money. But I remember *always* having this particular protective 'thing,' as if my mother maybe *knew* something was going to happen, or at least she wanted it to happen, I don't know. As soon as I began to show signs of any musical talent at all, via, I imagine, notes of enthusiasm or words of enthusiasm from my local piano teacher, whom I still adore, Mrs. Hattie V. J. McKenneth, I think that's when my mother began to believe that maybe I would become, you know, *something*."

"First you began playing the piano?"

"First I began the piano at a very early age. And then I started playing extremely well quite early—by about ten or eleven—and I was playing for all the Sunday school functions—all sorts of social functions the Ladies' Club would give for benefits, and little social affairs, you know."

"Was that for colored people only, or all people?"

"Oh, no. Completely white."

"Segregated?"

"Well, you see, usually a Southern town is made up of two units. That is, Negroes live in one section of town and white citizens live in another part of town. They are perfectly charming to one another. They meet in stores uptown . . ."

"But not in church?" I put in.

"They don't meet in church—it's a strange phenomenon, very strange. That's why it's so difficult, I think, now, because it's a strange phenomenon. They are actually friends in the strangest places, and enemies in the places that don't make sense at all."

"Let's get to yourself, Leontyne," I urged.

"O.K.," she said heartily, as if banishing a painful memory. "In a way, I remember very much that my father was terribly old-fashioned (and I'm very glad, in this stage of my life, that he was) when I got to courtin' age—which was considerably earlier than nowadays. They used to start about sixteen, because you really should have been married by eighteen."

"You were really an old girl if you weren't married by then?" I asked.

"Oh, yes," she said. "This highfalutin idea about going to college was a bit much, you know, so the idea that Mama had was that I was just not going to be in the local group; I was going to go through high school—preferably with honors, which I did—I was going to absorb as much as possible, if it meant mortgaging the house, which was the only thing my parents ever owned. Fortunately they didn't really have to go too far—well, yes, they did," Leontyne corrected herself, "because there was my brother, who was frankly, I find, extremely more intelligent than myself, who had to be fed, clothed and go to school, too. So I used to make a little extra money doing little piano jobs and things around town, and hither and yon. That's when I

77

began doing little soirée things up in what they called the Big House. In other words, on the hill—that's where the white citizens lived in Laurel, and I always played with the three Chisholm girls. We were about the same age. I remember the Chisholms had an enormously beautiful playground. My aunt's servant house was set on the premises."

"Is that how you got to know the Chisholms, through your aunt?"

"Yes. I used to go up to the Chisholm house and I would play for them and I think I was supposed to have a little thing going for me—I was rather bright, they said—and I used to dance or I would sing or I would play the piano."

"You sang, too?"

"I sang, too, but not much. You know, everybody sings down that way!"

"But you showed no vocal talent?"

"I would think that was too early."

"You weren't a child soprano, or anything like that?"

"No, but I was a *good* piano player; I still play piano fairly well. I had a very happy childhood, in a word. I was poor, but I had enough to eat and I had enough clothes to wear. I *liked* the world I had as a child. The main thing is that there was so much love *inside* the home that I was raised in. My brother and I are extremely normal—very close. My parents were not the kind of people who were afraid to show us that they were pretty stuck on us, and I think that has been a very good thing for me. My brother, who is a major in the Army now, wrote me recently what I think is one of the most beautiful letters from a mature American male I have ever read, which said that of all the men he had ever met in his life, including some officers in the Army he really admired, he still thought the man he would like to be like most in his life is our dad, and I think it's because we were . . . well, it's kind of like the Italian families, the provincial families. There is so much warmth and sweetness in the home. If there were problems, and there must have been many, I'm sure, it was all arranged very maturely—I have never heard my parents argue with one another. I have always seen my father treat my mother with the greatest respect, and sometimes even now I can see the strength of his love. Perhaps because she is younger than he, I don't know, he treats her in a very special kind of way. We just had a nice time as children, we really did." For a moment Leontyne Price lost herself in savoring her happy childhood.

"So you went to high school . . ." I suggested.

"Yes. I graduated from Oak Park, a vocational high school."

"Is that a segregated school?"

"When I was going to school it was, and it still is now, oh yes. That's frankly what makes this news, because that's the auditorium in which I sang about a year ago to a nonsegregated audience."

"How come?"

"Because I would not sing without its being nonsegregated—this is the strange thing about success. . . . It's an American story in a sort of a way, but it's sort of incongruous. I think people in Laurel and neighboring towns around, who knew my parents and knew me as a little child, skipping around, you know, playing for these little things, and whatnot, suddenly felt as if I were a part of them and, unconsciously, they didn't quite care whether they sat next to each other or not."

"It brought them together, you mean?"

"In one unit—in one hall."

"Because they felt that they had produced you?"

"Perhaps that *is* it—I don't want to sound immodest! But if that brought them together in one auditorium, I'm very happy."

"Now, how did you manage to do that if it was segregated? You made a condition that you wouldn't sing unless it were nonsegregated?"

"No, I didn't. I'll tell you the truth, I just said I would like to sing. I had another schedule completely changed at the Metropolitan for a release early in the season in order to do this concert for the benefit of this church in Laurel. This congregation had been trying, as long as I have been born they have been trying, to take care of that church, and every year they would say 'Perhaps next year,' you know. All through college it was still there, leaking and cold and whatnot."

"And they couldn't raise the money?"

"No! So the first time I went home I gave a concert, and there were white and black people sitting together and nobody paid any attention. This particular year, because of the Oxford situation, which was happening at the same time, it was suddenly completely newsworthy. I had all sorts of offers from magazines, you know, who print this kind of thing, and I begged them not to come with me. I begged them to stay away because I was positive that I would not sing to a segregated audience. I can't explain it to you. I had no guarantee. It was a condition with *me*, yes, I did state that, but that doesn't really mean anything in the South, it could always go wrong. It didn't."

"And this took place while the Oxford thing was on?"

"Right at the same time."

"And nothing happened?"

"Not one thing. As a matter of fact, a white cop helped my aunt, who is eighty-two years old—the one who worked as a servant for the Chisholms—helped-her across a mud puddle and, as a result, I think she will die happy, I really do! And the entire thing was handled with extraordinary taste simply because nobody was self-conscious about it. I think that's why."

"Well, you did it, and I'm sure it was because they felt they had had some part in producing you."

"May I also say something which may make you feel good, or which may embarrass you," Leontyne Price said, blushing. "If it does, I'm sorry. You see, ever since 1955 there was this particular thing that happened in Laurel, a tremendous recognition of the local girl who made good up North. That's all right. It's not so unusual. But if it's done by a big organization like NBC, which was the year that you-all took that chance and let me sing *Tosca* on your TV Opera—that's when the building of this particular faith and this particular relaxation about seeing me, personally, as the local girl, do practically anything paid off. Sure, some stations cut me off, but what happened? I came back to NBC the next year in *The Magic Flute*. After that I did *Carmelites*. The people in Laurel are completely relaxed about seeing me do anything, so that when I do a debut in the Metropolitan, which is recognized also in the South as our big opera house, they are very used to seeing me do perfectly normal things on the stage. In other words, I have a feeling that this, too, helped start this sort of national pride about me, you see. So, although they would not forget that I am a Negro—they *cannot*, that's painfully obvious—I do think that because of their sort of civic pride in me, and

81

seeing me in 'big time,' as they would call it, for so long, they really didn't stop to think about it being anything but the thing to do."

"Yes, your 'big time' then became Laurel's 'big time.' "

"I really think that's true."

"You didn't tour with the Met, did you? Or did you?"

"I did last year."

"Did they go South?"

"We went to Dallas, Texas."

"Was it desegregated?"

"It was desegregated. As a matter of fact, I never will forget it. I did *Fanciulla del West*, and I had this marvelous horse which was sent out by Neiman Marcus, the department store—it was really a marvelous horse and I'll never forget it, because the two stagehands, who were white, had to help me on the horse. So I was riding around a little bit, and they said they kind of got a kick out of the fact that I got a big bang out of riding this horse. And suddenly, I didn't think it was kind of strange; it was a real kind of a show. Outside there were Negroes and whites going in together, which, actually, Mr. Bing had already said was going to happen. The Met doesn't sing to segregated audiences. There may be trouble with hotels, but they do not sing to segregated audiences, so there was no trouble about that. But the main thing that happened to me was that there was one of the janitors backstage who wanted to get my autograph."

"A white man?"

"No, a Negro gentleman. So he said, 'If you stuck around here a little while you really would change a lot of things. I never thought I would live to see tonight!' "

"Isn't that wonderful!"

"And, personally, he was extremely proud of me. He didn't know me but he was very proud of this particular situation, you know."

"You graduated from high school with honors," I said, wishing to get back to her career.

"Yes, with honors. As a matter of fact, I had two scholarships, but they were both to local Southern schools, colleges very near my home. I don't know what got into my dad, but he just didn't want me to go to any Southern college. So I got a scholarship to Central State College in Wilberforce, Ohio, and that's where I graduated from."

"How old were you?"

"I was seventeen years old."

"Had you sung then at all?"

"Yes, I started singing then."

"Did you study—or did you just sing?"

"No, by then I was playing and singing. I was really a local success!"

"What were you singing?"

Leontyne laughed out loud. "You'll die," she said. "Things like *Homing*, 'All things come home at eventide . . .' and *Because*. *Because* was really my hit tune, because I was really the wedding and funeral girl of all time! Any time anybody died or got married, you know (in those days I don't think we had a telephone) they would just run over and say 'Somebody's getting married,' or 'Somebody died.' "

"Did you get paid for this?"

"Well, not very much."

"Now, when did you begin to study singing?"

"I began to study singing in 1948, September 1948, at Juilliard School of Music."

"How did you get to Juilliard?"

"Well, my first two years at Central State in Wilberforce I majored in Music Education, which meant it was kind of a security."

"You could get a job."

"I would have graduated with a degree in public school music and I would have been able to teach in schools—that was the whole thing. I had to be that practical for my father. But by my third year I had started to sing for local things—in chapel, in the glee club—and I started singing more than I was playing because, oh, I don't know; but when I started to sing people would listen. Then President Wesley started having me sing when the dignitaries would come—like the Ohio Board of Education members and visiting dignitaries from other colleges. I was always up there singing in my basic black dress! I'm afraid it was *Homing* again, but I had worked up *Vissi d'arte* in English—I'd rather not go into the translation—and I was always singing *Depuis le jour* in English, and I sang things like, well, all the hit tunes from the *Messiah*, you know."

"You sang *Depuis le jour* without having studied?"

"We had a coach there; her name was Catherine Van Buren."

Leontyne is most careful to give credit to everybody who has ever helped her.

"Did anyone think you were remarkable as a singer?"

"Dr. Wesley did. Technically, that's when I got my application for Juilliard, because he sent for it himself. I graduated from college, fortunately with honors—I was *cum laude* in my class, 3.6 average—and by the first of my senior year I had decided: O.K., I'll take a chance on it. The summer of my junior year, the Chisholms went down

84

to my father—that's why I will always respect them—and asked him if it was all right for them to finance my going to New York, because I talked at great length about my future with my parents and with the Chisholms. Mrs. Chisholm by this time was really sort of my confidante—I listened to records at her house and I was exposed to a lot of things."

"Had you sung in her house?"

"Yes, I had sung in her house since I was little, you know. Played the piano and stuff like that."

"Were both Mr. and Mrs. Chisholm convinced that you had a very fine voice?"

"They were very enthusiastic. In one word, the Chisholms said to my father that they did not feel that I should stay at home and teach in the Oak Park school, and would my parents give their permission for them to finance me. My father is a very strange man. He does not like to owe anybody a nickel—and I respect the Chisholms tremendously because they came to know him as a person, and they spoke to him like an individual, and I think that is why that relationship has maintained itself. I graduated from Central State College in Ohio the summer of 1948, June, and I came up to Juilliard because my application had been accepted, but you had to come up a week early, you see, to audition, and I did. I'll never forget—it was September 13, 1948."

"The 13th! That was taking a chance, wasn't it?"

"Right. But it wasn't a Friday!"

"The Chisholms financed your trip?"

"They financed my trip and they paid for my board at International House—my food, my books. International House is right across the street from Juilliard. It's a marvelous place. I'm a better person for having lived there. It has foreign students and American students living in the same building."

"So you went and had your audition and you got a scholarship?"

"Yes. I also received a job on the information desk at International House, which helped. I think I made about, after taxes, twenty bucks a week. That's enough to help you get by on. And the Chisholms paid all my board and my food and my books. And I studied with Miss Kemble."

"Then what happened?"

"Well, I got the opera bug when I came to New York, because I remember the first performance of opera I ever saw was at the City Center. It was *Turandot*. Then the second performance I went to did it for me. I stood up at the Met to hear *Salome*. I was completely gone then and I said to myself, 'I have *got* to be an opera singer!' It was very difficult to get into the Juilliard Opera Workshop, because you really have to have outstanding qualities; there's not that much room in an active opera workshop in a school. So sometimes students waited as long as three years to get in. Finally, in my second year I got into the Opera Workshop and I did my first role—it was in *Gianni Schicchi*."

"You sang Lauretta?"

"Oh, God, no! I wasn't nearly enough of a star to do Lauretta. I was one of the aunts—Nella. And then the next year, which was my last year there, suddenly I was asked to do Mistress Ford in *Falstaff*, and, pow! I still have the review from the *New York Times*—by Olin Downes! It was a public performance and it was a wonderful performance, and that was the first time that Robert Breen,

86

Blevins Davis and Virgil Thomson heard me sing. All three were at that performance up there, because Blevins Davis and Robert Breen were planning to do a production of *Porgy and Bess*, and Virgil Thomson asked me to do Saint Number Seven in *Four Saints in Three Acts*. That was the first professional check I ever got, for the Number Seven Saint. Everything started to happen at once after *Falstaff*, for some weird reason or other. Since I was not a regular student, you know, a student who was pursuing an advanced degree—although I could have, as I was getting enough credits—I withdrew from Juilliard when I did *Four Saints in Three Acts*, because to draw Equity pay you must get out of a student category, or something, and that was my first big break. We went to Paris, with *Four Saints*, for the Congress for Cultural Freedom. That was my 'big time,' my first trip to Europe, in 1952. In the meantime, before I left I signed a contract to do *Bess*, which they were planning to open in Dallas, take to Philadelphia, then to Washington, then to Berlin, to Paris and London. That, of course, is where I met Mr. Warfield, who was the Porgy to my Bess. I guess I must have gotten infatuated or something, because I ended up getting married, you see, to Mr. Warfield. We were married in 1952, August 31, and left the next morning for our Berlin tour. So we were in Europe until the following February, and then we played ten months at the Ziegfeld Theatre here in New York. Then Mr. Mertens of Columbia Artists heard me, and that's the way that change came. Mr. Mertens wanted me for recital touring and he signed me immediately for recitals. So in 1954 I made my Town Hall debut."

"What did you sing?"

"I sang a very esoteric program. When I think of it now

87

I get goose pimples. I opened with *Grands Dieux* from *Alceste* and I did an early Italian concert aria, I've forgotten the name of it now. Then I did a German group. I did a group of vocalizes by Stravinsky, songs by Rachmaninoff and Samuel Barber. Oh, it was way out—a way-out program."

"How were the reviews?"

"The reviews were mixed, but all in all, I came out pretty well. There had been a lot of excitement about my run as Bess at the Ziegfeld, so a lot of people came to see how I would bridge the gap, because that's not usually done; it's like sort of going from Ethel Merman's *Gypsy* to the Met, and that's a long way. And I was all cleaned up for the job. So one day Maestro Peter Herman Adler, who was the musical director of the NBC-TV Opera, came to a performance of *Porgy and Bess* and he was particularly impressed by the long good-bye to Porgy before I go to the picnic, where I sang a sustained pianissimo which went down to nothing, and he just went out of his seat; so then he called to find out who was handling me and so he found out, and then he brought you to me."

"You to me!" I corrected jokingly. Leontyne looked crestfallen.

"Me to you. I'm sorry. Peter brought me to you at your office at NBC. It was summer and I had on a blue checked dress."

"I remember that dress very well."

"You were very charming to me. I was kind of innocent and sweet in those days."

"Well, you still are."

"I must say I was scared to death because you had a very official look."

88

"I thought you were a charming, pretty girl, and I didn't think you had to sing even," I said gallantly.

"Oh, my God, you go too far!" Leontyne exploded. "Well, he brought me to you and I didn't really know what was going to come from it all. At that time I didn't know all the things you had to discuss, about the difficulties; and naturally it was involved because you had all the problems with the Southern stations. You said when I sang for you, I'll never forget: 'This is the sound we want, and we're pleased to have you with us, Miss Price, et cetera, et cetera, and we hope that you will be pleased working with us. You will be a wonderful Tosca.' "

"And I can now disclose to you that I wasn't in a position actually to take the responsibility for putting you on the network as Tosca."

"Let's face it," Leontyne said cheerfully, "it was the first step."

"Yes," I said, "it *was* the first step, so I had to go upstairs and see Mr. Sarnoff and ask him if it would be all right with him. And Mr. Sarnoff said, 'Is she a good singer?' and I said, 'She's a *great* singer,' and he said, 'That's all you have to think about.' Yet after all that we ran into a lot of trouble with some of our Southern stations."

Leontyne's eyes glistened. "Do you know," she said, "I didn't know anything about that until the whole thing was finished."

"There was no sense in worrying you."

"And this was to me the beginning of my professional career—my opera career. Well, everyone involved at NBC has become a dear friend. And one thing that was most important is that I learned professionals really don't have to be difficult to get something accomplished. You could have a very relaxed atmosphere, and *mountains* are chopped down because everybody is so pleasant. When I got out of television and started in the professional theatre, I found out it's exactly opposite—it is completely the opposite. Through NBC, and one of your productions—it must have been, I think, *The Magic Flute*—came my technical American on-stage grand opera debut at the San Francisco Opera in 1957. It was in Poulenc's *Dialogues of the Carmelites*."

"You did the *Dialogues* first in San Francisco before you did it with us?"

"That's right. That's how I got my debut."

"Do you remember, Leontyne," I said, "a rehearsal of *The Carmelites* at NBC when I asked you if you could sing a certain phrase without taking a breath?"

"I was purple, but I . . ."

"And you said, 'I'll try.' "

"I said I was purple!"

"And you tried and it was absolutely heavenly—without any strain of any kind."

"Those were the days!" Leontyne chanted, like an "Amen" at a revival meeting. "And I learned one thing that is invaluable to me now—that all the action has to be done with the face, and with smaller gestures. And it's just the opposite in La Scala, or at the Metropolitan when, if I do something that is natural and real, the main thing is it can be seen by the audience in the big theatre."

"It's underplaying," I said, "and the big opera houses don't understand it."

"Television was really a school for me, because actually it was for television that I learned *Aïda*. I coached with Peter Herman Adler and Ludwig Donath—particularly the score of *Aïda*—and when I went to do *Aïda* with the San Francisco Opera I knew it upside-down.

"You know something? Two of my biggest breaks came when two operatic sopranos had emergency appendectomies! In 1957, in the middle of the intermission during something like the third performance of *The Dialogues of the Carmelites*, at San Francisco, suddenly the manager came in looking kind of strange, saying Miss Antoinette Stella had cancelled for an emergency appendectomy. They had all the little things there for *Aïda*, with no *Aïda*, and they asked me did I know it, and I said yes, I did, because I did, I really did—and the next thing I knew I was on the stage doing *Aïda!*

"I also remember something that was so funny. Wait 'til you hear this. I remember I had everything thought out in *Aïda*—I said to myself, I can't go wrong, this'll be the first time I've ever been out on a stage for this kind of thing, and let's face it, my skin was in my favor for a change; I got that made, I can't lose! There's nothing to worry about. O.K., fine: Molinari Pradelli is not a heavy-handed conductor; I will be heard. The only thing I don't know is exactly—well—if I get on the wrong side of the stage I *get* on the wrong side of the stage! I can't go wrong. When the Ethiopian slaves come in I will just go where they go; and with Robert Merrill, the Amonasro, I'll just go with him. But I did not see how they were going to change the Amneris scene into the tomb. I couldn't figure out where the tomb was going to be. So I kept walking up to the director, during the night, you know, between the acts, and I kept saying, 'Maestro, where . . .' but he acted as if he wasn't listening and said, 'You were wonderful; you are beautiful tonight; and you just go and change the costume and it's going to be fine.' And I said, 'I have a question to ask you,' but he said, 'Bravo, bravo, the first act! Bravo, bravo!' I said, 'Look, I have a question. Where is the tomb? Where am I going to die? I don't have the slightest idea where I am going to die!' And he broke up with laughter. Well, I did find the tomb.

"In 1953 I auditioned for Von Karajan in Carnegie Hall, and in 1958 he engaged me for *Aïda* in Vienna. From Vienna—I was a little timid in Vienna—I went to London. Then Cerquetti, who was to sing *Aïda* in London, had an emergency appendectomy!"

"You live on appendectomies!"

"Suddenly I was in Covent Garden. It was marvelous. Then, from that I got an offer from the Metropolitan, which I promptly turned down. Why? It was the wrong time, the wrong contract, and I was doing something else. Well, I was crying and getting advice from two or three people, and I forgot all about being the first Negro to be a Tosca at NBC, the first to be Pamina at NBC—all that went out the window. You know how such things happen, and I just thought, 'Oh well, I can't go now, so I'll never make the Met.' So I kept going back to Vienna because Karajan *liked* my *Aïda*. The next year I did *The Magic Flute*, in a German accent so Southern that Eric Kunz, who sang der Vogelfänger—the Birdcatcher—said, 'I just won't do *The Magic Flute* with you any more, Leontyne, because you are getting all the laughs. Pamina isn't supposed to get *any* laughs.' You have never heard anything like my German in *The Magic Flute!* But, you know, the Vienna press —well I never got such rave notices in my life. They said Pamina hadn't been sung that way in I don't know how long; and they were really kind of cute about the dialect.

"Karajan also invited me to Salzburg—that was in '59—and I did, for the first time, in my first year at Salzburg, Beethoven's *Missa Solemnis*. Then everybody got very excited in Salzburg, vastly excited. I must say it was sung well. The next year I was invited to do what you might call the hair-raising Mozart bit. It was sort of like the day I was brought to you, because Karajan said, pointing to me, 'That is who I want for Donna Anna in Salzburg next year for the new production of *Don Giovanni*. I sang Donna Anna in Salzburg and a few counts and baronesses and princes and princesses in the audience all dropped their lorgnettes and what-not, and it was just sensational.

"And it was after that that I was *properly* invited to the Metropolitan. That's when I had a decent contract offered me—it was 1960."

"You made your debut as Leonora in *Trovatore*."

"I did. There are only two parts that I have a ball singing—that I can just skip through—Leonora in *Trovatore* and Donna Anna in *Don Giovanni*. Well, that's about it. That's the story." Leontyne took out a compact and began doing her face.

"Now, what do you see in the future, if anything?"

She did not speak for some time, and I could see from her expression that she had left her career far behind her. Then she looked at me earnestly. "I would like to try to make a gap between this constant tearing at . . . no, that's not what I mean." She was struggling for words. "I would like to fulfill a little more of my personal life. By that I don't mean I want to find a knight in shining armor on a white charger, or something. I know that already I have made the choice I want to make. But I'm in my mid-thirties, and I'm a little bit too young to be quite so pre-

93

occupied and narrow-minded about what I am doing. I think I would like to, at sixty or let's say fifty, not be so pre-occupied with whether my high C is going to come out or not, but really try to do something for somebody else. I have become very interested in doing something for the unfortunate youth of the city, and sharing what I have without being paid for it; to be available for things that may help people—"

"You think you have been a lucky gal, is that it?"

"I think I have had more than my share of luck, and I'm young enough to be able to enjoy the material things."

"But you would also like to pay back?"

"In some way I would like to show my thanks, I think maybe to God, for what he has done for me."

"Well," I said, "that brings me to the Negro question, and I would like you to talk about it because I think you have done a great deal to establish the pride of the Negro race. What do you think of the present situation? What do you think of the future? What do you think about what's going on, and what do you think ought to be done?"

Without hesitation Leontyne Price began to enunciate her credo as a Negro, an American, a member of the human race, simply, sincerely.

"I think the greatest country in the world is having growing pains," she said. "It has come at the time that it should have come. I think my people are right—we are right because, for one reason, we are finally prepared. No group at all, minority or not, no matter what color they are, can actually be strong if they are not prepared. These opportunities have been afforded in the only place they could be afforded—in the United States of America. The United States of America is having labor pains because of a new growth, a new dimension to the most perfect example of what democracy should be—the only country that makes an effort to have it this way. There are Europeans who have gone through absolute hell to be here to enjoy, to even die, in this country. Well, the blood of the black man is in the soil of this country. But this time there is no way out. We are prepared, and whenever a person is prepared it means several things. It means he is able to be responsible for himself. It means he is able to take his own mistakes maturely. It means that he is able to take freedom and have it and handle it in the way it should be handled. And I am very, very proud to be alive during this particular time. I know that the greatest hope of the world is for the growing pains of my country right now to solve themselves, which they ultimately will. In any minute way that I can I shall help, because everything involved in my life is completely American, and this has been a great joy to me. I do not believe in violence to solve anything. But I think it's the last chance for American democracy. It's very important; because if this doesn't prevail, then we're cooked. There's no escaping it now. That's why I say if this particular operation, this particular, what I call *delivery*, if this particular new child is not born completely normal, we . . ."

Words failed her. There were tears in her eyes. Leontyne smiled, opened her out-sized handbag and sought for her compact again.

"Have I talked too much?" she asked. "I've got to watch myself. You know, talking a lot isn't good for a singer." She was regaining her natural buoyancy. "Well, I must be going," she said, rising. "I'm leaving tomorrow for Rome, and I've so much to attend to—lawyers and things, and my hair washed and all."

She embraced me. "I wish you'd come over to Rome to

see my little flat, it's really only a hole in the wall, nothing like this," waving a hand at my walls as if calling attention to some vast, luxurious structure.

"And imagine!" she said with a mischievous smile, as I opened the hall door. "*Seven* nuns are my next door neighbors. It could only happen to me."

RICHARD RODGERS

RODGERS IS AN UNASSUMING, neat-looking man with a gentle, even warm manner. He and his attractive wife Dorothy live in a duplex apartment on Park Avenue. The elevator man who takes me up seems fully aware of Rodgers' importance, for he doesn't descend and keeps his eye on me until the composer's door is opened, I am unhesitatingly admitted, and he is satisfied that I am no intruder. The Rodgerses themselves are in the vestibule to greet me. I ask to be shown the rooms, and I am impressed with their size and furnishings.

"We've lived here eighteen years," Rodgers tells me, as his wife discreetly vanishes, leaving us to our interview. "It seems quite a large apartment now that our two daughters are married and on their own. It used to be just right when they were children running up and down the staircase and making lots of noise. Yes, it's too large now." He looks through the door of the living room at the staircase in the hall. "I escorted the girls down that staircase on their wedding day," he says cheerfully. "At any rate," he adds, "it's a good place for accommodating our pictures. We love pictures. You can see we have many, almost all Impressionist."

I walk with Rodgers through several rooms and look at paintings by Matisse, Vuillard, Picasso, Bonnard, Chagall,

Degas, Lautrec, Dufy, Pissarro, Renoir, Sisley, Vlaminck, Rouault. None of the pictures is run-of-the-mill. If it is a landscape, it isn't the usual landscape. If it is a portrait it is an unusual one.

"We have just bought two new ones," Rodgers informs me. "They're in my study." I follow him into his study. The newly purchased paintings are a Picasso abstraction of a guitar or some such instrument, and a Rouault of a ballet dancer. I am surprised at the new Picasso, for on the opposite wall hangs an early Picasso of a charming girl in yellow.

"I generally don't go for Cubist painting," Rodgers hastily explains. "But this Picasso attracted Dorothy and me. It is modest and quite decorous in color, don't you think? And it isn't aggressive, as so many such things are."

I agree that the Picasso is not aggressive, that it is even pleasant. Rodgers laughs quietly (he does everything quietly) as he watches me looking from wall to wall and comparing the very different styles of the two Picassos.

"Can't you hear," he says, "the yellow girl saying to the guitar across the room, 'Who would have thought that thirteen years later Picasso would be doing you!' "

I also wonder at Rouault painting a ballet girl.

"Yes," Rodgers echoes my thought, "it's quite a different Rouault, a happy Rouault. He generally paints melancholy people with large, penetrating, soulful eyes. Notice the ballet girl's skirt, how thickly the paint is put on. Rouault himself built and painted the frame, so that it is almost a part of the painting."

It is plain that Richard Rodgers is excited by the unusual. And as we return to his study I lead him into speaking about the unusual in his own field. I ease him into the subject by way of television.

100

"Today," I tell him, "I received a copy of a letter you wrote General David Sarnoff about NBC's production on television of Gian Carlo Menotti's new opera, *Labyrinth*. I produce NBC's television operas, so a copy of the letter was sent down to me. I am happy that you appreciate our efforts to put what is called serious music on television. I am glad you liked *Labyrinth*. But I can't help wondering why you, the finest composer of musical stage plays—you needn't shake your head, I think you are the finest—are sufficiently interested in television to write letters about it?"

"I am surprised at your question," Rodgers replies. "I am as interested in television as I am in live musical theatre because it may well be that the future of musical plays lies in television. It isn't with me a question of how good or how bad television now is. What fascinates me is the way the tools that belong to television are being used. Years ago I felt the same way about moving pictures. Larry Hart and I— Larry was my lyric writer from 1920 until his death in 1943—went to Hollywood feeling that the potentiality of the screen, its tools, could add a new dimension to musical theatre, a dimension it could not have on the stage. Larry, the director Rouben Mamoulian and I made a picture called —don't laugh—*Love Me Tonight*. And in that picture we found we could carry a song from place to place without disturbing its continuity. That is, the singer could begin the song outdoors and carry it indoors without interruption. In other words, we utilized the tools of the screen. I would gladly do a moving picture tomorrow, but it would have to be different from any musical play the screen has so far done. I am eager to experiment with any medium that would extend the scope of the musical theatre.

"Television!" he went on, mildly indignant. "Hell! I'm

on television many hours a day with *Victory at Sea* and the Churchill series, *The Valiant Years*. And don't forget *Cinderella*, the television operetta I did with Oscar Hammerstein a few years ago. The television medium is very important in my life because of its possibilities. For all I know there will come a time, and soon too, when all amusement, all theatrical art will be confined to the home screen—to television. And I want to be prepared for that time by familiarizing myself and experimenting with all the facets of television. Television is an art form even though not all of what you see on it is good. I have no patience with people who look down on television simply because it offers mostly mass entertainment. There is nothing wrong with mass entertainment, but I should like to help raise its level. The live theatre produces plenty of bad plays, but nobody claims that the theatre is not a form of art. There are plenty of bad instrumentalists, vocalists, conductors, composers, poets, novelists and painters, yet no one says that the media these people work in are not forms of art.

"You know, I look at the Johnny Carson show three to four times a week. It goes on at eleven-thirty at night and lasts till one A.M. I get into my pajamas and watch it from my chair. The informality of such shows intrigues me. I begin to see possibilities for the musical theatre in such an approach. I try to be open to everything. That is really what life means to me—curiosity, change. And I want to be a participant in change, not just an onlooker, an accessory *after* the fact. I think I've been like that always. At least I hope I have."

Richard Rodgers has been "like that" as far back as 1925, when he and Lorenz Hart wrote the first *Garrick Gaieties*. I myself had the good fortune to be present at the opening

102

night, and I now recall what a delight the show was, how refreshingly new and charmingly sophisticated. Rodgers listens immovably as I speak about the *Garrick Gaieties*, and I imagine he rather undervalues the show as an early product. I am obliged to point out to him that a song like *Manhattan*, one of the highlights of the first *Garrick Gaieties*, was unusual for its warmth, its insouciance, its gay acceptance of the less glamorous aspect of city life. *Manhattan* was quite different from the stereotype of a city song, the pumped-up raptures about Broadway or Park or Fifth Avenue.

"Now tell me what street compares with Mott Street in July?" Hart wrote, and Rodgers created a tune that matched the tongue-in-cheek query, evoking a steaming, colorful Chinatown in midsummer and, indeed, presenting it so melodiously, simply and artfully that one felt an urge to repair at once to that hitherto alien thoroughfare to revel in its blistering temperature and delightful atmosphere. In effect, Rodgers and Hart slyly nudged us to look around and find pleasure in *all* our surroundings, in *all* the levels of our existence, much as Cézanne and Van Gogh made us aware of the beauty and charm of objects hitherto unperceived by us or ignored—the lowly apple and the lowlier potato, a rustic bedstead, an ordinary cane chair, a framed lithograph hung awry. Rodgers smiles faintly as I go on. He seems rather uneasy at my scholarly, elaborate estimate of an early effort.

"Well," he says, "I don't know if *Manhattan* is as important as all that. And I'm overwhelmed at your comparing my little song with the art of Cézanne and Van Gogh. I think you're trying to be kind. But I can tell you that even at the time I wrote it—I was only twenty-three—I didn't want to do the usual thing. And a funny thing—because I

103

was not altogether satisfied with what was done in the musical theatre before me, though I admired a good deal of it—everything that happened to me was strictly against the rules."

"How do you mean? What rules?" I asked. And Rodgers in his quiet way—he never raises his voice—said, "It's easier for me to illustrate what I mean than to explain. Let me begin by telling you something about my family and my upbringing.

"By all the rules of musical romanticizing my family should have been poor. They weren't. We were, in fact, unfashionably comfortable. My father was a doctor with a fine practice. He could afford to give his children a good education. I went to college—Columbia. Now in the case of a musician who was destined to write many hit songs and earn a lot of money, the rules have it that he must be born poor and struggle to get an education, or else go without one. Another rule is that parents of a future successful musician must frown on his ambition and put every obstacle in the way of his gratifying it. We broke both rules. I was actually *weaned* on music. My mother was a first-rate pianist and a wonderful sight reader. I must say, however," Rodgers added parenthetically, "that she had the dimmest notions about popular musical theatre. She would say to me, 'Why don't you write something popular like *Yes, We Have No Bananas?*' I never studied any instrument, but I always played the piano by ear, and I still do. I can play anything by ear. I started composing when I was about fourteen. At fifteen I wrote an amateur show for a boy's club benefit—to raise money to buy cigarettes for our troops overseas. We had just entered the First World War. I learned how to compose by composing. I composed a lot, and I conducted my own shows. At seventeen I wrote my first Broadway show. (*Poor Little Ritz Girl* it was called.) I composed it at the piano and I had to have it taken down by someone who knew notation. In those days it cost about fifteen dollars to have a song taken down. Just figure out how much it would cost to take down a whole show. I couldn't afford it. So I had to learn notation and take my songs down myself.

"In my sophomore year at Columbia I decided to go all out for music. I quit college and went to Juilliard, where I studied theory—my major subject—with Percy Goetschius, the noted musicologist and theorist, and I attended the lectures of the then well-known music critics William J. Henderson and Henry Krehbiel. My father paid my first year's tuition. I got a scholarship for my second and third years."

Rodgers chuckled. "Nowadays I manage to reverse the flow. I am on the board of trustees at Juilliard, my favorite board; and I give scholarships. See what I mean by 'against the rules'?"

I thought I saw.

"Now as to the *Garrick Gaieties*," he resumed, "that project was certainly strictly against the rules. The Theatre Guild had built its own theatre on Fifty-second Street and they needed tapestries to adorn the walls. Well, Theresa Helburn and Lawrence Langner, the Guild's guiding spirits, asked me and Larry Hart to put together an entertainment which would be given twice only—a Sunday matinee and evening. They would ask friends of the Theatre Guild to buy tickets, and they hoped they could raise enough money to buy a couple of tapestries. And because the Guild was then at the height of its popularity and influence, the newspaper critics were invited to come, and they came. Why was I asked to write the show? Accident. My father had a patient

105

who was the Guild's lawyer. Benjamin Kaye was his name, and it was he who suggested me to Miss Helburn and Mr. Langner. What happened was again against the rules. We should have received bad notices and have succeeded in spite of them. We didn't. We received good notices and succeeded.

"Because of these good notices the show was repeated the following Sunday night. I was twenty-two years old and quite nervy. I went to Miss Helburn and said, 'Why don't you let us have the Garrick Theatre for a run?' I knew quite well that the Lunts were playing the Garrick in Molnár's *The Guardsman*. Miss Helburn said, 'What'll we do with *The Guardsman?*' And I said, 'It's been running for a year. Close it.'

"Miss Helburn didn't even gasp at my effrontery. She said quite calmly, 'I'll tell you what we'll do. You take the midweek matinees—four afternoons—and if you do well, we'll close *The Guardsman* and let you have the theatre.' 'Good enough,' I said. And that June week, the hottest of the year (remember it was long before air-conditioning), the four matinees were sellouts. Miss Helburn kept her word. She closed *The Guardsman* and gave us the theatre."

"And the Lunts?" I inquired. "How did they take it?"

Rodgers beamed. "The Lunts," he said, "were darling about it. A year later I had three hits running on Broadway—*The Second Garrick Gaieties*, *Dearest Enemy* and *The Girl Friend*. I composed the music. Larry wrote all the words."

I wondered, never having known him, what sort of man Hart was, and how he and Rodgers got together.

"A wonderful man, and a marvelous lyric writer," Rodgers said. "According to the rules we should have met by accident. I ought to have stumbled across him in a doorway or some such place. But I didn't. Hart needed a composer. I needed a lyric writer. A mutual friend introduced us. Simple as that. Hart and I worked together for twenty-four years."

Rodgers heaved a nostalgic sigh for the twenty-four fruitful, vanished years and asked me to have a drink. He went to a little bar in a corner of the room, looked for the ice bucket and, not finding it, went out to fetch it. After a prolonged time he returned with a single glass in which rested two cubes of ice. "The stuff doesn't agree with me," he said, explaining the absence of a glass for himself.

"You had three hits running in 1926," I reminded him as he sat down again facing me.

"Yes. Also in that year Hart and I went to London and wrote a show called *Lido Lady*. It was a big hit."

I said I didn't recall seeing *Lido Lady* in New York. Rodgers brushed *Lido Lady* away with a wave of his hand.

"Oh," he said, "we didn't bring it to New York. Why? Because we had no respect for it. It was one of those English synthetic jobs—to put it kindly. In other words, it was no good. Many years later we wrote *Jumbo*, and Billy Rose produced it at the old Hippodrome. Remember the Hippodrome, where the chorus girls would walk into a water tank and disappear? I considered *Jumbo* important because it was the first time a circus was used as background for a musical show. And it was a successful musical score. Several of the numbers in it became standard pieces. The next milestone? Almost immediately after *Jumbo* came *On Your Toes*, and that was the first musical show to use ballet. Not interpolated ballet, but ballet as an integral part of the show. We kept on writing shows—a flock of them. *Pal Joey*, *By Jupiter*. There was a revival of *Connecticut Yankee*. Hart died five days later." He sighed again, then brightened. "And we were lucky. We had had, until Larry's death, only one flop.

"I first met Oscar Hammerstein when I was a boy of thirteen. Later we were classmates at Columbia and I wrote one song with him for a varsity show. In 1927 Oscar wrote the lyrics for the now classic *Show Boat*, but since that triumph he had had a series of failures. Discouraged, he retired to his farm at Doylestown, Pennsylvania, and wrote no more. When Hart became ill and it became clear that he would never write again, I drove out to the farm and said to Oscar, 'You and I should begin to think of collaborating.' The Guild people had been talking to me since the *Garrick Gaieties* about my doing an *American* show, saying there had been no such thing in the musical theatre. I said, 'Great! Send me an idea.' They sent me the play *Green Grow the Lilacs*, a Theatre Guild production which had not done too well. But we saw its possibilities, and it certainly was American. Oscar and I went to work. We hit it off together immediately. No strain. No adjustment period. I had a ball, and I guess Oscar did too. *Green Grow the Lilacs* became *Oklahoma!* Up to date, it has been seen by more than fifty-five million people. I have the figures in my office."

"And *Carousel* followed *Oklahoma!*"

"Yes," Rodgers said. "But I must tell you that Oscar and I didn't like the story at first. Lawrence Langner and Terry Helburn had suggested it, and they worked on us for seven months before we gave in. Funny, isn't it? It's my favorite score."

"My favorite," I put in, "is *South Pacific*. And my favorite song in *South Pacific* is *Younger Than Springtime*. It's a gem. It is pure and innocent and lovely as a lilac."

"I'm glad you think it pure and innocent," Rodgers said

earnestly, "because we meant it to be just that. Consider the story at that moment. A young and handsome naval officer on a South Pacific island is presented, for a consideration, with a beautiful, very young Polynesian girl by her im- moral, money-grubbing mother, called, most appropriately, Bloody Mary. The two young people are left alone in a tent. From my standpoint the situation was perilous. I was up against a problem of taste. The young lieutenant could take advantage of his bargain. On the other hand, he could take the curse off the transaction by poetically succumbing to the beauty and innocence of the young girl. The first would be crude and ordinary, the second poetic. We took the second way and wrote *Younger Than Springtime*."

"And turned what could have been a sordid episode into a lovely, innocent expression of romantic youth," I added, and went on with my enumeration of the Rodgers-Hammerstein successes. *"The King and I . . ."*

"Ah!" Rodgers said. "That was a rare case of a musical show coming after a movie version. . . . *Flower Drum Song* was a big hit. So was and is *The Sound of Music* and *No Strings*. Now, in *No Strings* . . ." Rodgers paused. "But you haven't seen *No Strings*."

I confessed I hadn't.

"Please do me the favor of seeing it, because in it I think I have gone a step further in enlarging the scope of the musical theatre. We'll talk some more after you've seen it. Call my secretary and she'll get you my house seats. Her name? Just call Nancy. Never mind her last name. Just Nancy. She's a dream secretary—she knows everything and anticipates everything, and she's no eyesore either. I can't stand ugly people around me, can you? Have another drink. I'll go and get some more ice. And next time let's meet at my office. I want you to see my office. It doesn't much look like one. It's really a satisfying set-up."

I went to see *No Strings*, and some days later I presented myself at Rodgers' office on Madison Avenue, where I was conducted to a large, comfortable living room. There was a grand piano at one end. I asked Rodgers if he did his composing at it, and he said, "Oh, no." The telephone rang and, excusing himself, he talked business over it. His secretary came in with letters. "That's Nancy," he said. And to her, appealingly, "Must I sign them?" Nancy said sweetly, but firmly, "Yes."

When she left, Rodgers said, "You see why I don't do my composing here. Composers, like other people, are creatures of habit in their work. I am used to my study at home, where I'm not interrupted. I play the piano, I scribble down notes, I stop, I drink a cup of coffee, I read a book, I wander through the house, I talk to Dorothy. . . ."

I told him I enjoyed *No Strings*, and I congratulated him on his courage in tackling head-on the problem of race. It had never, to my knowledge, been done before in a musical play.

"Well," Rodgers said, bristling, "I don't want to sit on my tail" (he used a more expressive word). "I'm too old to do that."

"You seem always to have been too old to do that," I said. "You certainly didn't sit on your tail when you wrote *Oklahoma!*, *South Pacific*, *Pal Joey* and *Carousel*. Each one was an advance for the musical theatre, and each was, if I may say so, a morality play. When I consider your work as a whole I find that you are really a moralist and philosopher in musical clothing. Certainly only a moralist, humanitarian and philosopher could have set before audiences used to the lighthearted, uncomplicated, orthodox romantic fare of the musical theatre the grim story you pose in *No Strings*, in which a Negro girl and a white man fall genuinely in love and kiss and embrace and sing beautiful romantic songs about each other. And the effect on the audience the night I saw *No Strings* was unmistakably uplifting. Perhaps a parallel to you in the nonmusical theatre would be George Bernard Shaw. He also used entertainment as a tool for presenting his political, social and economic ideologies."

Rodgers blushed. "What company you keep putting me in!" he said. "But I do try to put whatever talent I may have to further what I consider liberal and good. I happen to believe in the old-fashioned virtues. I believe in having one wife. Dorothy and I have been married thirty-three years. I believe in the goodness of average people. And I am by nature optimistic."

He suddenly leaned forward and said with a quiet intensity, "If I weren't, I should probably not be alive today. Seven and a half years ago I sat in the chair you are sitting in and pounded the desk in a fury at Dorothy, who was sitting on that sofa there, sobbing hysterically. We had just come from my doctor, who had told me that I had cancer of the jaw. I was furious with Dorothy for giving up without a fight, and I shouted, 'How dare you!' I was not frightened—oh, not at all—"

"How could you be sure? . . ." I murmured, interrupting, inwardly marveling at such fortitude and optimism.

"Oh, no!" Rodgers went on, "I was not frightened, not at all. I just wasn't ready to die. You know, I worked that whole weekend. I wouldn't let them cut me up until I put

111

Pipe Dream, the show we were going to do, in rehearsal."

He laughed.

"It would be nice to tell you that *Pipe Dream* was a great success, but it wasn't. It was a flop. But success or flop, I was *determined* not to die. I was *sure* I wouldn't. The doctors put a great deal of weight on my attitude. Don't look so skeptical. A patient's frame of mind has much to do with his chances of recovery. My brother, who is a surgeon, tells me he prefers not to operate on pessimistic patients."

Rodgers nodded several times to dispel whatever doubts my look must have expressed. His own face grew relaxed, and he presently looked serene, as if his fearful ordeal had never taken place. I noticed that the surgeon—probably with the spiritual aid of the patient's confident belief in recovery—had done a beautiful job of reconstruction on the composer's face.

"A funny thing," he went on, "I now find the appetites more urgent than when I was young. I am more interested in people. I have a *compulsion* to live. It could, of course, be a sign of encroaching age." He smiled disarmingly. "But it also could be a sign of encroaching maturity, don't you think? I find it in every department of my life. My eye is more receptive. You can see it on my walls at home. The Lautrec is one of the first things we bought. But now I have more modern, experimental pictures—three Dubuffets and a Riopelle. Upstairs there's a Hans Hofmann—he's a modern American, as if you didn't know." (I didn't.) "There's a Graham Sutherland, he's a modern English painter. Now why does one start buying these things? I think because there is a maturity of interest, that instead of one artistic target one has many.

"I know fellows of my age who are unbearable. They

are repetitive. They drink too much. Their sense of humor is gone, and they seem to secede from life much too early. Their ambition is to spend the rest of their lives on the golf course. Unfortunately, many of them get to the fifteenth hole and drop dead. Why, at my age, should I take on the job at Lincoln Center, the management of the new theatre for operetta? Why? Because if it comes off it will be the realization of my hopes for the American musical theatre. It will give it the place it deserves in our native culture. Physically, geographically and aesthetically it will stand between Philharmonic Hall and the Metropolitan Opera House. That is as it should be." Rodgers' face was glowing with anticipation of success.

"How do you mean, the place it deserves?" I asked. "The American musical theatre has always been successful, hasn't it?"

"Perhaps you're not aware of it," Rodgers answered, "but there's a curious snobbism that claims music can't be good if it makes money. Yes. You'll find this snobbism in the press, and especially among composers—the so-called serious composers, I mean."

I reminded him that Brahms had said that he wished he had composed the *Fledermaus* of Johann Strauss, an operetta which had from the first made money and is still making it. Rodgers was unimpressed.

"Well," he said, "in America at any rate, the musical theatre is generally considered a whore. My one ambition is to help make a good woman of her. You know, because I am not included in the category of 'serious' composers, I was kept out of the National Institute of Arts and Letters for years. While the whole country was singing and whistling my *Some Enchanted Evening*, I wasn't considered a qual-

113

ified practitioner of the arts, while some 'long hair' who hadn't a melody in him, but had a smattering of the cacophonous procedures of modern so-called music, was rapturously welcomed into the National Institute of Arts and Letters. For myself, I know no substitute for melody."

"Neither did the great composers from Monteverdi to Stravinsky," I put in. "I'm told your daughter Mary has inherited that gift from you."

"She writes lovely songs," Mary's father said quietly, attempting unsuccessfully to conceal his pride. "And now you are going to ask me the standard question: 'Is your daughter jealous of you?' And my answer is that she has no reason to be. She's strictly and quite successfully on her own. Her attitude to me has been one of 'Don't tread on me,' that is, 'Don't be inquisitive, and don't try to influence me.' The fact is I never heard a note of her new show until I went to Washington for its first performance. She never asked my opinion of it. I rather like that," Rodgers said, this time with unconcealed pride. "My younger daughter Linda is a fine pianist. She often gives chamber music evenings at which she plays. I have, so far, never been invited. Well, I understand my children. They want to be independent no matter if it hurts us. That, too, is as it should be. And we owe them our grandchildren. Mary gave us four; Linda one. We are very grateful."

On the way out Rodgers showed me various rooms in his suite where much of the Rodgers-Hammerstein business is transacted. One very large room was completely lined with shelves which held the scores and parts of the firm's innumerable shows. A number of men were busy in this loft-like room. One man sat at a table obliterating with an electric eraser the markings conductors, singers and instrumentalists had left on the scores and parts. That action appeared to be his sole duty. I was told that at the moment sixty-six sets of the score and parts of *Oklahoma!* were in circulation, which meant that sixty-six productions of the musical were in rehearsal or being performed. The monetary returns from all the rental and rights fees of all the past and present shows, often with the addition of a percentage of the gross box-office take, were startlingly huge. Rodgers' earnings seemed to me more than sufficient to justify his exclusion from any and all fraternities addicted to the practice of Arts and Letters.

When we descended to the street it was rush hour. "Let me drop you," Rodgers said. "I have my car and chauffeur waiting. Oh, I'm living it up, all right. I'm very grand indeed!" he added apologetically.

We got into his car and began a slow progress uptown.

"You must be making millions," I said indelicately, as I reclined in the luxurious, resilient back seat beside him. "But you have to give most of it to the government, don't you?"

He turned to me and said simply and seriously, "I don't mind. Look, I really like it. Because of it I could bring up my children without fear. I live very well, I'm afraid of no man, and I can say what I please. That's a pretty good return for my money, don't you think?"

I thought it was.

ARTUR RUBINSTEIN

ARTUR RUBINSTEIN LOVES MUSIC. Offhand, this seems like a ridiculous statement about a famous and much beloved artist. The general opinion is that all musicians love music, but I have had a lifelong association with many noted and popular musical performers, and among them I have found very few who were not indifferent to music. The reason is rather obvious. Performing artists master their art (or in some cases, trade?) at an early age, and by the time they have achieved fame and a career, music has become an old, an unexciting story for them. Though they must continue to practice a good deal in order to keep in trim and meet competition, they seldom play, sing or conduct for pleasure. And outside of their own specialty they appear to have little, if any, interest in other performers and in other forms of music.

Rubinstein seriously and passionately loves music and music-making. He goes to other people's concerts as often as his own busy schedule permits. Most often, performers attend concerts for some purpose other than pleasure. The widow of Enrico Caruso once told me that her celebrated husband occasionally attended a song recital or an opera performance in order to gauge the merits or the demerits of a possible rival. He and Mrs. Caruso would slip into gallery seats, so as not to be recognized, and remain until the great tenor could estimate fully the abilities of the man he had come to hear. That never took more than about ten minutes. Caruso, his wife recalled, invariably left the hall or the opera house with a smile of satisfaction on his face.

Artur Rubinstein is not concerned about possible rivals. He is ready and eager to listen to fellow artists or to make music himself at any hour of the day or night. He loves chamber music, and he has found the secret of blending the percussive tone of the piano with the lyric tone of the strings. When the music is for strings alone, he listens enraptured. One day, after a performance of Schubert's *String Quintet* at a private house, he was so moved that he went up to the first violinist and handed him, with every evidence of emotion, five twenty-dollar bills. "I felt I had to do something to express my gratitude for such divine music and such a beautiful performance," he said apologetically.

"I cannot tell you," he tells me, "how much I love to play for people. Would you believe it—sometimes when I sit down to practice and there is no one else in the room, I have to stifle an impulse to ring for the elevator man and offer him money to come in and hear me? I am happy to play to a crowded Carnegie Hall. But I am just as happy to play for a thousand people, for three hundred, for a hundred, indeed for anyone who cares to listen. Just look at this schedule." He showed me his engagement book for the coming summer, so penciled in with names of cities that it looked like a railroad schedule. Most performers rest in the summer. Rubinstein, after a taxing winter of concerts, booked himself solidly for a summer tour of Europe, playing almost daily. It is a schedule that would strain the endurance of the youngest artist. Rubinstein, who admits to seventy-three, is certain to take it in stride and come through exhilarated.

Now he sits facing me in the library of his duplex apartment on Park Avenue. His face is still boyish, and his puckish smile, with a suggestion of harmless sophistication, reflects his ageless vitality, awareness and hedonism. He has just returned from a long recording session; he should be dog-tired, ready for supper and bed. But he isn't at all; or, if he had been tired earlier, he no longer is. The prospect of talking about music has revitalized him, and he says he is ready, even eager, for a long evening with me.

I remind him that I first heard him play in Mexico City some forty years ago, long before he made a name for himself in the United States. The house was packed and the audience rose in a body and cheered when he came on the stage. At the end of the program there were shouts for *Navarra, Sevilla, Cordoba* and other pieces by Albéniz, all new to me then but favorites with the Mexican audience. Hearing him play this music, I realized that the youthful Polish pianist had an extraordinary command of Spanish rhythms and Spanish musical coloring; indeed, his playing of Spanish music was the recognizable expression of the nation's soul. He was made to play countless encores, and when the concert was finally over, he was carried to his hotel on the shoulders of hysterical Mexicans. When I returned to New York and reported this astonishing triumph, someone jokingly remarked that the Mexicans probably thought they were hearing Anton Rubinstein, not Artur.

Laughing at his own expense at this anecdote, Artur Rubinstein tried to explain to me the reason for his success in Mexico. "Very early in my career I showed an affinity

121

for Spanish music. In 1916 Spain adopted me, you know, in the way America adopted Paderewski. I learned things very quickly in those days. It took me three weeks to learn all the twelve pieces of Albéniz' *Iberia*. Albéniz did not know the resources of the piano too well, and he wrote often in an awkward way. So I had to fix up his music to suit my fingers and to make his unpianistic Spanish vignettes 'sound,' as we say. Have you tried to play *Navarra* as Albéniz wrote it? You'll find it impossible. It is not only finger-breaking, it is ineffective. The same is true of Stravinsky's *Petrouchka*. Stravinsky wrote a piano version of *Petrouchka* especially for me, and this, too, I was obliged to fix up. Well, the Spaniards were enraptured, also the South Americans and even the French, with the way I played Spanish music. But I must confess that, while I was happy to give pleasure with Spanish music, my heart really belonged more to the classics, old and new—to Bach, Mozart, Beethoven, Schubert, Schumann, Chopin. It also belonged to the impressionists, to Debussy, Ravel and our Polish Szymanowski. I spent years introducing the music of Szymanowski when his name was hardly known outside of Poland."

Rubinstein's speech, like his piano playing, is alive with nuances. What he says is always spontaneous, his ideas and opinions are his own, never second hand. His broad, humanistic culture is a rarity in this age of specialization. It comprises a knowledge and appreciation of the history and the arts of many diverse civilizations. While now a citizen of the United States, Rubinstein is more a citizen of the world. He is equally at home in New York, Warsaw, Paris, Rome, Madrid, The Hague, Brussels, Monaco, Jerusalem, Lima, Buenos Aires, Rio and Santiago; and he used to be at home in Berlin before the Germans took to the grisly practice of genocide.

There is hardly a major language that he does not speak fluently. He uses his hands vividly, and his dissents are generally and amiably prefaced with, "But my dear fellow," in the English manner—and he makes the phrase sound persuasive rather than patronizing. As you listen to him and watch his graceful, illustrative gestures and scan his curiously shaped head with its receding tough, curly hair, his sharp, small, probing eyes, you feel the presence of a man absolutely different from the generality, a throwback to a once elegant, original species, now extinct but for him. He is, indeed, or appears to be, the sole survivor of the poet-musician type, a blend of charm, naïveté, sophistication, knowledge and genius, the type forever symbolized by Liszt.

"When I look back on my life," Rubinstein said reflectively, "I see myself as two men, one different from the other. The man before, and the man after, marriage." I recalled catching sight of the first man, the bachelor Rubinstein, in a Paris restaurant many years ago. It was the night of the famous Quatre Arts ball. On that night, as on St. John's Eve centuries ago, or in the *Fasching* season to this day, all the accumulated restraints of civilization may be discarded, the celebrants permitting themselves freedoms normally prohibited or frowned on. Rubinstein (accompanied by Jascha Heifetz) wore a bizarre armless, full-length garment, underneath which one caught glimpses of his white skin. Persons equally unrobed or disrobed wandered in, seemingly unconscious of their strange appearance. Unorthodox behavior by the students and their guests at the ball was hinted at in the next morning's papers. It was reported that, in the early hours of the morning, Rubinstein and Heifetz stopped on their way home at a night spot in Montmartre, took over the chores of the establishment's violinist and pianist and played for hours to the patrons' delight.

"Those were happy times," Rubinstein mused wistfully. "How different from the strained gaiety of today. When we dance these days, it is in desperation, as if over a volcano, really a *danse macabre*, an uneasy dance like Ravel's *La Valse*. And you know, my dear fellow, this feeling of a volcano beneath us is the reason our modern composers write the way they do. They are afraid of life and they take refuge in noise, in sterility, in destruction. They ignore the soul of man, which has not died but has been temporarily obscured by a cloud; they write from panic, to keep from feeling anything. It is the same nowadays in all the arts.

"But the true artist does not ignore the soul, no matter what the outward state of the world may be at the moment. In the darkest years of the czars the great Russian artists—Pushkin, Lermontov, Gogol, Tolstoy, Turgenev—celebrated the Russian soul. Flowers grow even from a dung heap. The true artist is always an optimist because he is dealing with the soul of man, not the superficialities of life. And all true art is romantic because the divine essence of man is forever mysterious, forever beautiful. Does this sound banal to you? If it does I can't help it. I know no other way to say it. And I'll remind you that it is proclaimed in all romantic music. Of course it is said there better than I say it to you.

"An artist *knows* that life is romantic, because anything at all may happen. You remember that song in Rodgers' and Hammerstein's *South Pacific?* I forget what it is called, something about looking across a crowded room and seeing, unexpectedly, for the first time, the girl of your dreams. You know, my dear fellow, though that is a romantic idea, it is what one always hopes for. Any evening may prove to be the enchanted one. Every day may bring adventure. I have felt that way all my life. That is why I love to go out. There is always the possibility of meeting someone who will open a new window on the world, the commonplace world you've known. Just as there are no two fingerprints alike, so there are no two persons alike. I have known many great and important men and women in my time who have contributed immensely to my understanding and appreciation of life. The mailman, the cook, the charwoman—I find these exciting, too, for they are highly individual, each one of them, and each has a point of view different from the others and from mine. Yes, I find most people exciting.

"I am so busy living my life that I can't seem to find time to write about it. If I ever do an autobiography I shall call it *A Fairy Tale*, because that is what it has always been. It is a fairy tale right now. Even before I was born something remarkable happened to me. Let me tell you about it. I was my mother's seventh child. My mother did not want a seventh child, so she decided to get rid of me before I was born. Then a marvelous thing happened. My aunt dissuaded her, and so I was *permitted* to be born. Think of it, my dear fellow! It was a miracle. And as if to show my gratitude for my debut in the world, right away I began to show an aptitude for music. You see, I wasted no time. When I was a year old, believe it or not, I could carry a tune, and at four I played the overture to *Poet and Peasant* four hands with my sister—you know that delightful, melodious piece, so seldom performed nowadays, that goes Tah-tah-ta-ta-ta, ta-ta-ta? On my fifth birthday somebody presented me with calling cards on which was printed 'Arturic, pianist virtuoso.' Arturic was my family's pet name for me. I was, of course, enchanted with the cards and passed them around freely to friends and even strangers. You see, I never had any false modesty. I was sure of myself. I had perfect pitch—indeed, I had everything necessary for a musician. But you know, I was not really interested in music. I have to confess my ambition then was to shine in baby athletics!

"My uncle, who was a very cultured man, saw my musical possibilities and felt I had no time to lose, that I couldn't begin my career too soon. So at four he arranged for me to play for the famous violinist Huberman. Huberman was impressed with my playing and wrote a letter to the great violinist Josef Joachim, in Berlin, telling him all about me. And, fairy tale again, the great man wrote back a long letter warning my uncle that a talented child must not be forced. 'Don't,' he cautioned, 'make a monkey of him; and see to it that he listens to good music only, especially to good singing, and don't let him take lessons before he is six.' Joachim ended the letter with a hope that I could be brought to Berlin to play for him."

Here Rubinstein's face broke into an amused, a dimpled smile.

"Fairy tale again," he continued. "Listen. It so happened that my sister was about to be married. In those days Polish people considered Berlin—not Paris—the proper place to buy the bride's trousseau, and my mother was taking my sister to Berlin to buy her one. I was taken along

126

to meet Joachim. And that, my dear fellow, marked the turning point of my life."

In Berlin, Joachim received little Arturic cordially and put him through a severe musical test. He made him play a tune in several keys. Then Joachim sang the second theme of the first movement of Schubert's *Unfinished Symphony* and asked the boy to improvise an accompaniment. This Rubinstein did without hesitation. Joachim was enthusiastic and suggested, rather whimsically, that the lad be taught the violin. When the Rubinsteins returned to Lodz the boy was given a violin. But Arturic had no patience with the instrument and smashed it to bits at the earliest opportunity. He willingly took piano lessons, and at the age of six he gave a charity concert, playing among other things a Beethoven sonata, a waltz by Chopin and Mendelssohn's *Spinning Song*. When he finished the printed program he improvised.

Soon the child Rubinstein outgrew the pedagogic opportunities of Lodz and was sent to Warsaw to study at the Conservatory. When he was ten he was sent to Berlin again. He was now sufficiently advanced to be regarded as an artist. Joachim openly took him under his protection and put up his own funds, along with contributions from three Jewish bankers, to finance the young artist's education. Arturic studied with Heinrich Barth, a pupil of von Bülow and a severe teacher. Barth's pupils usually left the classroom in tears. Once he dismissed a young American student with "You wouldn't have me swindle your parents, would you?"

In those days Berlin was the stronghold of the partisans of Schumann and Brahms. Like Barth and Joachim, Rubinstein declared himself on the side of the classicists and

127

against the revolutionary romantic school of Wagner and Liszt. When he was eleven, Rubinstein made his Berlin debut with Mozart's *A Major Concerto*, Joachim conducting the orchestra. At the same time he pursued his studies with Barth and dutifully attended the rehearsals of the famous Joachim Quartet, and thus, early in life, learned to know and love the classics of chamber music. But he distinctly recalls falling asleep at a performance of Beethoven's *Quartet, Opus 131*. "I still do," he added.

Rubinstein's mother wanted her son to be brought up under the refining influence of feminine society, so in Berlin she placed him in a pension for girls. Artur took to the refining influence with a vengeance. He acknowledges (with a twinkle in his eye) that to this day he has not recovered from that influence. Like Lord Byron, who fell in love at the age of eight, the twelve-year-old Rubinstein promptly conceived a passion for a girl of twenty, who lived at his pension. In an effort to bridge the disparity in their ages, Rubinstein, unaware at that time of the leveling power of his art, sought to become proficient in more manly pursuits, such as riding a horse. After many lessons and several falls, he paraded his new accomplishment before his lady love, who, Rubinstein recalls, was annoyed rather than impressed, and hardly deigned to look his way. When his passion was discovered by the management, his "inamorata" was asked to leave, and Rubinstein lost track of her.

Twenty years later she visited him backstage after one of his concerts. The pianist choked with emotion on recognizing the object of his childhood infatuation. "Now occurred another miracle," he says, with a fervor that annihilates the forty years that have passed since that reunion. "The lady spoke of my youthful passion and confessed her past infatuation for me. The disparity in our ages did not now seem so serious an obstacle as it had before. I guess that was the miracle."

Reverting to memories of his youth, Artur Rubinstein sadly shakes his head at his irreconcilable states of mind at the age of sixteen. Piano playing came easily to him. "Therefore," he says, "a pianist was for me a very inferior being." A composer was several cuts above a pianist in his estimation, but a formidable obstacle stood in the way of his composing music. "I was too good a musician to compose second-rate music," he confesses, "and it was not easy to be first-rate." Worse yet, he found himself constantly in love, and obliged to devote much of his time to the problems and anxieties of that imperious emotion.

At the same time he could not help being caught up in the musical war that raged so violently in the capitals of Europe at the turn of the century. It was a conflict that parted friends, set father against son, teacher against pupil. The cleavage was sharp; one was either for Wagner, Liszt and Richard Strauss, or for Schumann and Brahms. To be for all five was unthinkable. For a youth of sixteen the choice was clear. Notwithstanding his obligation to his teacher Barth, and to his sponsor Joachim, Rubinstein now espoused the cause of Wagner, Liszt and Strauss.

His protégé's rebellion against classicism did not disturb Joachim's faith in Rubinstein's talent, and he continued to use his considerable influence to further the young man's career. Through Joachim's good offices Paderewski invited Rubinstein for a visit to Morges, Switzerland, where the celebrated pianist lived in baronial splendor. Paderewski received his visitor cordially and presently

129

asked him to play. Rubinstein was nervous and played badly, but his host sensed his quality and pressed him to stay a week. At a large party he gave one evening, Paderewski had Rubinstein play for the guests, and this time the youth played so brilliantly that "Le Maître," as Paderewski was called, kissed him on both cheeks.

Madame Paderewski, Rubinstein recalls with amusement, was less charming, permitting herself rude remarks about him, such as, "The boy eats well at table."

"She was right," Rubinstein adds. "I did eat well at table. And, if you've noticed, I still do."

It was, nevertheless, a most profitable stay, for among the guests at the party was the influential Boston music critic, William Foster Apthorp. When Apthorp returned to America he spoke glowingly about Rubinstein to the Knabe piano people, who thereupon arranged an American tour for him. Rubinstein was seventeen when he made his American debut.

"Yes," Rubinstein says, recalling those faraway days, "I suppose I *was* brilliant—how do you say, flashy?—as a pianist. Otherwise why should all sorts of people have engaged me to play in all sorts of important places? Astruc in Paris signed me up for five years, and I made my debut there in a notable series of concerts called *Les Grandes Auditions de France*. Mary Garden was the assisting artist, and she sang three Debussy songs in French with an American accent. These opportunities came, I think, prematurely for me. I was gay, always in love, and most disinclined to practice; so it really was not surprising that the critics said I was not well prepared. I wasn't. You know the *A Minor Étude* of Chopin, the fast one? Well, I played it and missed ninety per cent of the notes. But it was successfully *bra-*

vura, and it impressed the audience, though not the critics. My difficulty was that I had so much vitality and dash that I could get away with, as you say, murder."

At this point, Rubinstein's seventeen-year-old son Johnny came into the room and said, "Mother asked me to deliver three messages. First, you are to offer the chocolates to your guest. Second, how soon will the interview be finished? And third, shall the ladies come down?" The ladies were Mrs. Rubinstein, my wife and two others, friends of the Rubinsteins. The pianist, smiling, answered, "First, tell your mother I shall offer chocolates to my guest when I find them. Second, I don't know how soon the interview will be over; and third, the ladies may not come down just yet." The boy left, grinning. "Charming lad," his father observed. "He has a sense of humor, I think. Now, where were we?"

"You had just gotten away with murder," I said.

"Ah, yes. As I told you, in 1915 I went to Spain, and the Spanish people adopted me completely. I must say I played Spanish music in such a way that my audiences found it hard to resist me. And that, my dear fellow, was a tragedy for me. For people accept the artist who flatters their national prejudices, while they ignore the better things he ought to offer them. I gave them what they wanted in the way they wanted, and I had a big success. But there was a void in my heart. Musically speaking, I was leading a double life. At home, in my hotel room, I was a different type. I loved the classics, the music of Bach, Beethoven, and so forth. I knew I could—how do you say?—wow any audience with De Falla's *Fire Dance,* but I would rather wow them with Beethoven's austere *Hammerklavier* sonata.

131

"Like all persons who lead a double life, I was happy only on the surface. Outwardly I was a man to be envied. My facility on the piano was incredible, but my technique was questionable. I remember once, in Rio, I ran into the great pianist Godowsky in the lobby of my hotel. 'I'm coming to hear you tonight,' Godowsky said, beaming. I blanched. 'Please, please don't come,' I implored. 'It is impossible to fake in front of you.'

"As I said, outwardly I was enviable. I spoke many languages fluently. I was socially adaptable. Everywhere I was taken up by society. In England I received large fees for playing in private houses—two hundred pounds, in fact, which in those days was a large fee indeed. But I was too lazy, too comfortable to practice, and I dropped as many notes as I played. My second tour of America in the 1920's was a personal triumph and an artistic disaster. I knew everybody, I dined out, I was sidetracked by pretty girls and beautiful women, and all this took up so much of my time and energy that I neglected the piano. The critics sensed this and were critical—all but you, my dear fellow. You wrote kindly about me because you felt the artist in me, notwithstanding the dropped notes. I was distinctly *not* a success in my second American venture, and I assumed that I should never return.

"Well, I grew older, I had an ever-increasing success in Europe and in Latin America, and an ever-increasing ache in my heart for the pianist I wanted to be but wasn't. I had never thought seriously about marriage; marriage was a curtailment of liberty, of that happy condition in which one is not obliged to account for one's actions. Then, all of a sudden, something happened to me, something changed me, and I found myself wanting two things desperately.

"I said to myself, look here, Rubinstein, this won't do; you must, before you die, exploit your real gifts as a pianist. Suddenly, also, I began to dream of having a wife and daughter of my own. And these desires began to have some sort of interdependence. I reasoned that if I had a wife and a daughter for their sake I would want to be the fine pianist I longed to be.

"So, in anticipation of this future family, I began to practice the piano seriously. God should have punished me for have sowed my wild oats over such a long period. But God was at the moment kindly disposed toward me, or else He was busy elsewhere. To enable me to realize my dreams, He led me to marry a lovely, beautiful woman I had been in love with for some years. Most fortunately and unaccountably, she loved me too. In due course she gave me the daughter I longed for and also provided the orderly life a serious artist requires.

"I began to practice and study the piano wholeheartedly and methodically for the first time in my life. My wife, by her sympathy and her ministrations, to say nothing of her cooking—she is one of the world's great cooks—and our little daughter, by her presence, gave me the respect for my talent which I longed to have."

Rubinstein got up and made a fruitless search for the chocolates.

"Nela was a young girl when she married me, and I was forty-three," he went on. "It was a serious thing, my dear fellow, a courageous thing for a man of forty-three to marry a very young girl. It is one thing for her to meet the aging man at a party, when he is all dressed up, nicely shaved, his gray, diminishing hair combed and brushed, or to visit him after a concert, his face still aglow with the music of Beethoven or Chopin. But it is quite another thing for her to see him in the morning in his pajamas, unshaved, uncombed and bleary-eyed.

"Yes, my dear fellow, it took great courage for me to ask a beautiful young woman to marry me. Believe me, it is easier to play the whole of *Petrouchka* on the piano. But the result was magnificent, at least for me. I became the father of two girls and two boys, lovely children—by good fortune, they all look like my wife. I worked hard at my piano, and I went back to America quite a different artist from what I was when I last played there. The public took me to their hearts, and even the critics began to say kind things about my playing. Since my marriage, I live in a dream of fulfillment—as artist, as husband and as father. In short, my dear fellow, I consider myself blessed."

Johnny again appeared in the doorway. "You may tell your mother," Rubinstein said, anticipating his son's errand, "first, I can't find the chocolates, second, the interview is about over, and third, we are ready to receive the ladies."

Johnny vanished, and a moment later the ladies came down. Mrs. Rubinstein found the chocolates easily, and brought out other refreshments. Showing no sign of fatigue, Rubinstein entertained us with stories and anecdotes, all of them revealing his unflagging ebullience, his deep interest in people and in everything that affects them.

Himself an irrepressible romantic, he deplores the lack of emotion in youth today. Yet he understands its cause and refuses to blame the youngsters.

"Our young people laugh at emotion because of the sterile, difficult life of the world around them. The cruelty of this life is expressed in the cruelty and cynicism of our literature, our noisy, meaningless music, the emotionless abstractions of our art," he said with great seriousness. He has no hesitation in identifying the cause of the perilous state of the world and its deleterious effect on the creative spirit. "Germany is responsible for it all. The two wars they instigated have not only destroyed countless millions, they have also infected the souls of the survivors. That is why I deliberately lose myself in the generous, romantic, liberalizing creations of the great masters of music. And my success as an interpreter of this music—it would be silly of me to be modest and pretend I'm not a success, wouldn't it?—proves to me that beneath the cruelty and cynicism that have so infected the world, our need for emotional release is most urgent. You see, my dear fellow, I am an incurable optimist. I simply cannot believe that the culture mankind has accumulated is for nothing, that the soul of man is destructible, that our beautiful world is doomed to perish.

"As for myself, I shall go on playing as long as anyone wants to hear me, or until my fingers fail me and my heart dries up, or until I am attacked by dry-as-dust doctrinairism—you know, the sort of artistic disease that causes one to play as if a metronome was ceaselessly ticking off the time, the kind that substitutes the brain for the heart when you are playing Beethoven. I hate musical straitjackets and I never shall put one on. Johnny, have you done your homework? If not, you may excuse yourself. But first, I would like you to play for us. Johnny plays the piano rather well, I think. Johnny's sister Aline also plays the piano beautifully. She is not here, alas! She is away in college, studying—not too hard, I hope."

Smiling diffidently, Johnny went to the piano and played

Bach and Poulenc. His father watched him nervously, stealing glances at me to see my reaction. The boy played charmingly, with a limpid tone and excellent taste. "And now, off to your homework," Rubinstein commanded gently.

Johnny said good night, kissed his parents and went upstairs. "What a delightful boy," Rubinstein said. "So understanding, so sweet with me, and he does play the piano rather well, don't you think? Not that I would want him to be a traveling musician like his father. I don't believe he has the right temperament. I have no idea what he'll be, but it won't matter. I am sure he will be a good, kind man, and that is what really matters, isn't it?"

ANDRÉS SEGOVIA

I HAVE KNOWN Andrés Segovia, the world's foremost guitarist, for the last thirty-four years, yet he continues to astonish me by playing, looking, behaving and talking like my preconceived idea of a Spanish artist and gentleman. He is courteous, discreet, austerely enthusiastic in his speech, proud, anachronistically gallant and, above everything else, superbly generous in his attitude to people. Sometimes, after one of his concerts in Town Hall, when he has added eight or ten encores to a long program, and the avid audience has reluctantly left, and after he has greeted wellwishers and embraced friends backstage, I have offered to carry his guitar in its heavy, bulky case and hail a taxi for him. These friendly proposals he invariably refuses, insisting on carrying his instrument himself, and walking to wherever a taxi might be found at this busiest hour of the night. When he finds a cab, Segovia holds the door open with his free hand, ushers in his friends and enters last, being obliged often to dispose himself and his guitar next to the driver.

Several months ago, on a wet, cold morning, Segovia arrived at my Manhattan apartment for lunch—in respect to promptness he is not, I am happy to say, characteristically Spanish. He was protected against the weather by a heavy sweater under his jacket, a thick overcoat, high overshoes suitable for a Montana blizzard, a woolen muffler and a large Spanish beret. As he refused my help in shedding these elaborate trappings, I stood by and admired the beret; the size seemed unusual.

"*Per*mit me, dear friend," he said without a moment's hesitation, "to present eet to you."

I said I could not deprive him of such a generous head covering on an inclement day. "Ah, then," he said, not pressing the point, "I have another beret exact-ely like theese-a one hwich I shall leave with your doorman tonight when I shall have occasion to drive by here."

At sixty-eight Segovia is ample around the waist and has a fair amount of hair. His face is large; the eyes, glowing behind thick glasses, are soft, intelligent and emotional; the brows, bushy. He wore a gray suit, a ribbed shirt with collar attached, and a shoestring tie. We sat down to lunch but Segovia had hardly taken his seat when he asked my permission to use the telephone. "I weesh to spick weeth my *abogado*, lawvyer, you call heem, ees eet not? to aska of heem to post-a-pone our meeting today abhout my hincome tass," he explained.

"The tax is high in America, especially hard on artists," I put in sympathetically. He nodded sadly in agreement. "Very high," he said.

"More than in Spain?" I asked.

"Oh, in Spain ees *no*thing. Very leetle," he answered smiling. "Also een Eetaly. Een Eetaly I have believed eet is not fashionable to pay tass. Baht een Hin*gland* eet is high. Much higher even than een America."

He telephoned his accountant or lawyer, arranged a postponement of their meeting and resumed his seat.

140

"Do you remember your first interview weeth me?" he asked genially. "Eet was in 1928 after my debut in New York. I liv-ed in Central Park in hotel and I did-a not spick a word of Heengleesh. We had inter-*pret*or. You were very kind at that time, *bee*-cause the guitar was not then consider-ed a serious instrument een America. You wrote in your paper—the *World*, I believe—a very sympathetic ar*tickle* about the guitar and how I play *eet*. Eet was trans-a-late to me. Very kind."

"You speak English well now," I hastened to say. Segovia smiled and shook his head doubtfully.

"You know," he said, "hwhen I spick Heenglish I can only espress half of what I think, and the listener can only understand half of what I say. And theese ees becawse I submit to the principle of hwone of our greatest writers and philosopher, Unamuno his name, that we have to spick for-ever foreign langwidge patriotically bad, in order to please our countrymen, that ees, to *pre*-serve the superiorit-*y* of our langwidge."

Segovia's English is elegant and learned. It is inter-spersed with bits of philosophy and allusions to history, geography and the liberal arts. Yet he is rarely sententious. What he says is the result of self-education and personal observation. His manners have the elaborate simplicity of Don Quixote, though physically he more resembles Sancho Panza.

He now addressed himself to his lunch as to a rite. He appeared to favor one dish, and I urged him to try the others. He wiped his mouth delicately with his napkin and said, "A friend of mine say we must eat leetle of, and good; and out of what ees good, plenty."

The lunch over, Segovia took another sip of wine, and

141

without reluctance or protestation of modesty began his story. It was a lucid, orderly tale, deliberately told. It sounded like a carefully thought-out improvisation of a personal theme, and it put me in mind of the once popular practice among musicians of improvising on a given melody, usually ending up with a brilliant triple fugue.

"I was the son of a lawvyer who wanted me to be one more lawvyer in the world," Segovia declared, and I felt I was hearing the opening words of a novel written in the first person. "And, as in Spain there are so many lawvyers, a very weetty man us-ed to say that lawvyer in Spain could become anything—even the re*gent* Queen. And my father believ-ed eet. I contradicted heem by taking one of the most disreputable instruments in the world, in Spain, hweech once was play-ed only in the ta*verns* to accompany *lubric*—that ees the Spanish for, I think, lascheevious dances and sonks. I took the guitar and conceal-ed myself in the garden of a very kind neighbor, for to practice. You may ima*gine* how I had to struggle against my fameely, the friends of my fameely and heven my own friends." Segovia took another sip of wine to erase the memory of the opposition to his earliest attempt to conquer the lowly guitar.

"Tárrega was the master at that time, of the guitar," he continued. "But I was ten years old and I never heard of eem. Hwhy? Be-cawse he was leeving in the op-*posi*te zone of Spain, in Valencia, and I was leeving in Lin*ares*, though I was baptiz-ed in Jaén, becawse my fameely move-ed there and I spend my childhood in Granada town, hweech may be the teacher of beauty for any arteest, so beautiful eet is eetself. You must, dear friend, come to Granada sometime and see if I spick true.

142

"Hwhen I expected Tárrega to come to Granada, Tárrega he unfortunat-ely die-ed. Then I was halone to deescover, by comparison to the other musical instruments, the technique of the guitar. Many year later a friend of mine, very well-known philo*soph* and poet, Eugeni d'Ors his name, wrote, 'The sonk of the piano eet is a pro*sah*ic discourse; the sonk of the cello ees an ele*gy;* the sonk of the guitar . . . a sonk!' "

"Who taught you to play?" I asked Segovia. He gave me a beatific smile.

"I was my hown teacher and pupil," he replied. "And have been so all my life without serious quarrel with each other. I learn-ed to play guitar by observ-ing how the other arteest play their own hinstruments. For in*stance,* I had a sweetheart who was student of piano. Music did not inspire her very deeply. But she inspir-ed me very strongly. Very."

I said I thought the piano was different. Segovia acknowledged the difference. "Never-the-less," he explained, "by observing how she studied, and for in*stance,* the fix-ed positions (it may be the same words een Heenglish) I did also in the guitar, gaining strength and independence to my feengers. Also the scales, also the arpége. And hwhen I have already my feengers obedience to my weel, I found with great sadness that I had no reper*toire* to play. I can assume that hwhen the vocation is there we burn a-down all the ob-*stacles* weeth or weethout a teacher, against poverty or een spite of wealthy."

Segovia went on with his novel, or novelette, in measured, picturesque phrases that often sounded like archaic translations from the original Spanish. "In 1924 ees my first con-cert in Paris, in Conservatoire. Madame Debussy, the widow of the composer, attended the concert, and she invited to her box Paul Dukas who compos-ed *L'Apprenti Sorcier*, Manuel De Falla, Joaquin Nin, the philo*soph* Unamuno, Albert Roussel (I was playing a piece Roussel wrote for me the name hweech was *Segovia*) and my wife Ahdelah-*ee*dah.

"My wife she was very beautiful. She lik-ed very much to sit in the loge among the public, and to receive the ohm-mahdge of every*body*. But, after she has witness-ed my practicing and saw I had-a to repeat a hundred times the same pass-*sahdge*, she became scare-ed to death of my playing in publeek, and she never appear any more in the hall, but she remain always where I was resting een the artists' room. And as she use-ed to spick with great imagination, telling her thoughts more in im-ah-ges than in words, she told to Madame Debussy, 'Hwhen I see the leetle finger of the left hand of Andrés going here and there in the fingerboard I am afraid that eet will miss the note.' To my nest con-cert after that one, Madame Debussy sen' me to the concert hall for my wife a beautiful flower bunch with a card say-hing, '*Pour vous tenir compagnie pendant que le petit doigt s'aventure tout seul.*' Heen Eenglish, 'In order to keep you company hwhile the little finger venture alone.'

"Big *succ*-sess the Paris con-cert. The creeteecs say-ed Segovia deescover-ed the guitar for them. And I have to say that the manager who organize-ed the con-cert not only cover-ed his espenses but gave me one thousand francs, and theese was es-septional in the French world of music!"

The room had become overwarm. I removed my jacket and invited Segovia, who looked uncomfortably hot, to remove his.

144

"Thank you, my dear," he said, "I am ver' comfort-able as I am. The guitar had very leetle rep-ertoire," he re-sumed as if there had been no interruption. "I had to work bringing to the guitar music reeten for the *vihuela*— the an*cestor* of the guitar—and the lute, making tran-screeptions of other hinstruments and finally interesting the composers to hwrite for the guitar. They answer with such enthusi-asm that Turina Torroba, De Falla and, later on, Tansman, Castelnuovo-Tedesco, Roussel, Ponce, et chetera, collabor-ated with me in raising the arteestic level of my hinstrument.

"From France I went fearst to London. A professor of the Cambridge College who was also a musicolo*gist*, after he has attended my tenth con-cert in the season in London, and looking at the distinguish public hweech came to hear them say-ed to me, stammering, for he stammered, 'My dear Ah-Ah-Ahn-dr-dre-*drés*, there ees in your con-certs no mm-mm-more p-p-p-place for any mm-mm-more du-du-du-duchesses,' meaning that Segovia had become so fashion-able. Then I tour Europe every year. And finally, in the nineteen twenty-eight, I came to America for the first time. Mr. Coppicus was the man-a-*ger* who engage-ed me becawse Kreisler spoke highly about me, inciting heem to engage me."

Here Segovia paused to smile at a recollection that had presented itself to him. "A funny thing I now remember," he began. "Hwhen Mr. Coppicus and his partner Mr. Schang hwent to Europe they go to a studio of a great Spanish painter, Miguel del Pino, who hath made my por-trait. Mr. Coppicus ask-ed him the permission of bringing the painting to New York and exhibiting it in the window of a famous store in the Fifth Avenue. And before I arriv-ed later on for my first concert in New York I re-

ceiv-ed in the boat a wire-*less* from Coppicus asking me to
be dress-ed exactly like the portrait for the photographers
who would meet me at the pier. Of course, as I have always
been reluctant to publicity, I did-ent comply with hees
wish."

Segovia's eyes sparkled with amusement at outwitting
his manager's clever publicity stunt. But when he resumed
his story, the simplicity of his speech and demeanor clearly
indicated that for him the present interview had no relation to publicity. He was merely tracing for me the evolu-
tion of the once vulgar guitar into an instrument as
responsive to the demands of high art as the violin, viola
and cello. And since he was the key figure in this evolu-
tion he could not justifiably exclude himself from the
narration. Then, too, his own adventures in the musical
world, both in Europe and in America, had a documentary
quality.

"Hwhen I arrive in the United States I thought the first
concert I had to give should be in New York in a well-
known place like Town or Carnegie Halls. To my bad
syrprise I learn-ed that my first concert would take place
in a private home. Now, an arteest never should make his
presentation in such a way. My experience of young arteest
in Europe was that the hostess, when she had in her home
a well-known arteest, did not renounce to hinvite more
pipple than the cap-acity of the house allow-ed, and so
making the acoustics bad, the *ambience* noisy and affect-
ing the pride in the arteest of the freedom he must a-have.
I could not refuse to play because it was specif-i-ed in my
contract the number of concerts I must give.

"The secretary of Mr. Coppicus accompany me to the
place I have to play. I did-ent spick Heengleesh at that

146

time. I spoke a few words in German. The secretary also spoke a few words in German, but they were not the same words as mine. So our conversation die-ed in the beginning. We arriv-ed by train in Proctor, Massachusetts, a leetle village with bungalows and sidewalks in marble, and we went to a small house. I was given a leetle room to rest. At seven o'clock I had already put on the full dress, and they ask-a me already to take my hinstrument to begeen my concert. I came down to the leeving room, and with a very deep syrprise I saw only three per*sons* were waiting for my concert—the owner of the house, her sister and his brother. That was the audience. I had made a very short pro-gram beforehand. But I dida-not care for it, and I was playing with great pleasure for two and a half hours when I saw how those three pipple were true lover of music. Theese was the first time my guitar sounded in the United States."

Segovia is one of the few artists who enjoy playing in private. I could well understand how surprised and charmed he was to find himself performing before an audience of three at his first appearance in America.

I recalled that it was in the same year that he played privately for Toscanini and a few of the Maestro's friends. Segovia brought his little footstool along with the guitar and he devoted the entire evening to music of the classical composers, Bach especially. I remember Toscanini saying that the celebrated *Chaconne* for violin sounded better on the guitar as Segovia played it. Later, at supper, Segovia said it was quite possible that Bach's unaccompanied violin sonatas were first composed for the lute.

To this day, when Segovia comes to dinner I do not hesitate to ask him to play, because I know he takes pleasure

147

in playing for friends. Of course he never brings his guitar, and when asked to play he modestly declines, alleging the absence of his instrument. This is at once rectified by an offer from someone to fetch it. Segovia then charmingly gives in, and in fifteen or twenty minutes his guitar is in his hands and his left foot is resting on an improvised footstool of a couple of thick books.

We draw chairs and sofas in a circle around him, and some of us sit on the floor to get an even closer view of him. Segovia thoughtfully bends over his guitar. There is a moment of palpable silence as the quality of the music he is about to play is visibly foreshadowed in his brooding stance. He generally begins with old music, and this time it is a Bach fugue. At close range it is fascinating to watch the artist's chubby fingers negotiating the tortuous demands of the most exacting of musical forms with unerring accuracy. Only seeing and hearing him thus can one appreciate the stubborn, inhuman labor that Segovia lavished on what is really a limited, percussive music box, to make it sing like a Spanish angel and express with extraordinary clarity and grace the deepest emotions. Having moved his listeners— and himself too—with the profundities of Bach, Segovia is now in a mood to exhibit the romantic, national aspect of the guitar. We call for the rhythmic or languorous pieces of his countryman Albéniz, and are rewarded with *Sevilla, Granada,* and some other of the locally inspired music of the composer who first brought world-wide attention to the musical physiognomy of Spain. But when he is asked to play *flamenco,* Segovia refuses, although he is said to be a master at it, and enjoys it when it is played by others. For him *flamenco* is gypsy music; and unlike Tolstoi, who considered the music of the Russian gypsy and peasant the truest art, Segovia's attitude to *flamenco* is indulgent rather than serious.

For Segovia the guitar is indeed a very serious instrument, as he claims it is now for thousands of enthusiastic devotees in Europe, Asia, Australia, New Zealand, Africa and, of course, the Americas.

"The guitar is such a *suc*cess," Segovia assured me, "that they are teaching it in every major conservatory in Europe. Here in America, one-third or more of the public hweech fill my concerts is compos-ed of young pipple that want, many of them, to learn to play, to stoody properly the guitar. And I advis-ed the musical authorities of these country acad*emi*es, conservatories, universit*ies*, et chetera, to create curriculum for the guitar to satisfy the eager wish of the youngs to practeece that hinstrument.

"But, you know, I must tell you that the guitar is difficult hinstrument. Even now I must to practice fice to siz hours every day, even day of concert. I practice usually two hours in the morning. Then I stop. I take the bath. I take the shave and practice again. This means that I always practice with pleasure, with-out fatigue. Don't believe the artist who says they practice eight to ten hour a day. Either this is not true, or they cannot improve any more on their art. For the attention is tire-ed. The mooscle of the finger are tir-ed. And no thing good can be accomplish-ed in that state."

In view of so rigid and full a regimen I hesitated to ask Segovia what he does with his spare time. But he was not surprised at the question and replied that he finds plenty of time for his hobbies, which include reading philosophy, poetry, history and viewing works of art.

"And, although I have a sedentary life at seven hundred miles an hour flying over the globe to more than a hundred

149

concerts each season," he added smiling, "I like to swim and ride horseback. As for the ladies," he went on with a twinkle, "in Spain we have two symbols of man in love— Don Juan and Don Luis. They were competitors, but weeth this differ-*ence*, that women belong-ed to Don Juan, hwhile Don Luis belong-ed to women. I am not Don Juan," he admitted, shaking his head sadly.

I asked him what he had in mind for the future, and he answered without hesitation as if he had long ago settled the question that plagues all performers of a certain age. "To play less," he said. "To hwrite my guitar experience to help students, and hwrite an autobiography hweech weel be not as many autobiographies of others are, an index of *suc*cesses, but rather a kind of panora*ma*—panora*ma* is Eengleesh word, no?—a panora*ma* of music and art of our times, and how to put that out of the distress the art is suffering."

"Why do you say distress?"

"I say that the situa-tion of the arts—of all the arts—is now ter*rible*. For one good painter or sculptor or composer or poet there are thousand of mediocre individu-al who call themselves art*eest* without knowing nothing habout the speerit or the technique of their art, but only the commerce-ial issue of their enter-prise. My book will deal weeth this depressing sujjet. And I am late to publish it, for fear to be devour-ed by those medio-*crats*.

"The abstract painting and the concrete music!" he cried with the gentle alloy of bitterness that characterizes this aristocratic Spaniard's extreme of disapproval. "Both are denial of true art. There is a general cowardice among art*eests* and cree*teecs*. The art*eests* wanta the quick *suc*cess. Becawse of this cowardice we are confront-ed with authoriz-ed fakes in poetry, in painting, in sculptyoure and een music. The pipples in the museums should refuse the hospitality to mediocre painting. The musical arteest should refuse the hospitality of the concert stage. All theese I shall tell in book. Hwhy? Be-cawse I must."

Segovia rose. "I have say-ed, I think, everything I wish the public to know about the guitar, and also hwhat I believe to be the trouble with art today."

In the vestibule he sat down and painstakingly drew on his heavy overshoes, refusing my help. At last, secure against the weather from top to toe, he "embrac-ed" me solemnly as part of his never-changing ritual of leave-taking, and went away to keep his appointment with his *abogado*. He must have forgotten to leave a duplicate of his beret for me with our doorman. A month has already passed. But one day he will suddenly remember with horror about the beret, and he will hasten to my house and give it with an apologetic note to the doorman. "Dear Friend," the note is sure to read, "I am inconsolable for my forgetfulness, and I pray you to forgive me. An old man often forgets, and I am not exactly young. However, the proverb say 'Better late than never.' Please to accept the beret with my compliments. As you said, this beret is not the small unimportant kind one buys in Paris. It is a Spanish beret, big and noble. I shall hope to see you wearing it with pleasure. Your abashèd friend, Andrés."